CLASSIC BEER **10** STYLE SERIES

STOUT

MICHAEL J. LEWIS

Brewers Publications
Boulder, Colorado

Copyright 1995 by Michael J. Lewis

Copy Editor: Anne Higman
Technical Editor: Robert Letters
Book Project Editor: Theresa Duggan

Brewers Publications would like to thank the following people
from Guinness for their help during the technical edit: George Irons,
Park Royal Brewery; Michael Clarke, St. James's Gate; and Peter
Walsh, Guinness Museum at St. James's Gate.

Information for the commercial stout breweries in Ireland, England,
Scotland, and Whales, listed in the appendix, is from the *Real Ale
Drinker's Almanac* by Roger Protz (Info. Devel's Press, 1993).

Printed in the United States of America

10 9 8 7 6 5 4 3 2 1

Published by Brewers Publications, a division of the
Association of Brewers: PO Box 1679, Boulder, Colorado 80306-1679;
(303) 447-0816; orders@aob.org; and FAX (303) 447-2825.

Direct all inquiries/orders to the above address.

Cover design by Robert L. Schram
Cover art direction by Marilyn Cohen
Interior design by Vicki Hopewell
Cover photography by Michael Lichter, Michael Lichter Photography
Thanks to Boars Head Pub Supply for donating the glass for the
cover photo. For more information about Boars Head Pub Supply,
contact Doug Schuetz at (708) 234-9300.

Library of Congress Cataloging-in-Publication Data

Lewis, Michael, 1936–
    Stout / Michael J. Lewis.
        p.   cm. — (Classic beer style series ; 10)
    Includes bibliographical references and index.
    ISBN 0-937381-44-6 (alk. paper)
    1. Stout.   I. Title.   II. Series.
TP577.L485   1996
641.2'3—dc20   95-47401
                                                                CIP

Table of Contents

About the Author

Professor Emeritus Michael J. Lewis conducted the program in brewing science at the University of California at Davis for thirty years. He continues to be responsible for research, teaching, and public service at the university. His academic accomplishments have led to his selection as a fellow of the Institute of Brewing (London) in 1985, one of only fifty scientists worldwide so honored. In 1986 he received the Award-of-Merit of the Master Brewers Association of the Americas (MBAA) and in 1992 was invited to be a senior member of the Brewers Guild (London). Dr. Lewis has published more than one hundred scientific papers on brewing topics, mostly related to brewing processes, including yeast physiology and fermentation, the behavior of cereal grains, biochemistry of proteins, interrelations among enzyme systems, and sensory science. Dr. Lewis consults with brewing companies, including the emerging microbrewery industry; with companies who supply brewers' raw materials and equipment; and with government agencies. His expertise is new product development, sanitary equipment design and sanitation practices, and assessment of research programs.

Graduates of Dr. Lewis's program are well represented in the brewing industry, especially in the major North American breweries as well as in many small brewing operations; other graduates are brewing in Europe, Asia, Africa, and South America. An outstanding speaker, lecturer, and teacher, in 1990 he received the Distinguished Teaching Award of the University of California. He has lectured and taught courses by invitation in many parts of the world, including Britain, Canada, Mexico, Venezuela, New Zealand, Ireland, Japan, and Australia; he has returned five times to teach special courses for the South African Breweries. Dr. Lewis coordinates many short courses at Davis for different audiences within the brewing industry, through University Extension (UNEX) and the American Brewers Guild (the Guild). These include the accredited nine-month Master Brewers Program leading to an internationally recognized professional qualification in brewing science and engineering (the Associate Membership Examination of the Institute for Brewing), and the ten-week Craft Brewers Apprenticeship Program of the Guild. His efforts in research, public service, and teaching have made Davis as much a Mecca among brewers as it is among wine makers.

Dr. Lewis earned his Ph.D. degree in 1960 in microbiology and biochemistry at the University of Birmingham, England. While in England he also studied and taught at the British School of Malting and Brewing. He has served on the board of governors of the MBAA and is a member of the MBAA, the American Society of Brewing Chemists, the Institute of Brewing (London), and the Brewers Guild.

Acknowledgments

I am indebted to Ashton Lewis who wrote chapter 6, Brewing Stouts at Home. Ashton, an expert brewing scientist and practical brewer, has many years of home-brewing experience. He has gained extensive research experience at the University of California–Davis pilot plant during his M.S. studies, and has learned to teach what he knows in front of advanced classes on behalf of the American Brewers Guild. Those interested in home brewing should contact him, not me. I was fortunate to have available the expert services of Susan Langstaff, also formerly a colleague and M.S. student at UC–Davis but now in private practice, to work with me on the sensory research reported in chapter 4. She conducted the extensive tasting sessions and undertook the necessary statistical analyses of the data to make sense of the results.

I am also indebted to another Lewis, my own dear son, David Lewis. David wrote most of chapter 2, assembled the list of stout brewers for the appendix, and gathered more photographs and other illustrative material than could possibly be included. David is arguably the best economist and business strategist active in the microbrewing industry and owns his own company, the Berkeley Group, in Berkeley, California.

I sincerely thank all those brewers around the world who make stouts for adding something special to the panoply of beers. I would like especially to thank the brewers who responded to our survey and for their contributions. The data they reported and the views they expressed are recorded here as part of chapter 5. I am grateful to D. M. Lay, librarian at the Bass Museum, who provided information about the early stout brewing activity of that ancient and distinguished company. Of course, the dominant stout brewer in the world is Guinness and without the generous support of colleagues and friends at Guinness Brewing Worldwide Ltd., this book would have been a quite different one. Peter Banner, Rick Winel, and June Austin made significant contributions, but the book would have been less readable, less accurate, less complete, and lacking some intriguing insights were it not for the Trojan work of Dr. Robert Letters, formerly the Director of Research for Guinness, who did me the honor of agreeing to be the technical editor of the monograph. Some, but not all, of his contributions I have identified.

Finally, it is a pleasure to recognize the patient and thorough work of Elizabeth Gold and her staff at Brewers Publications. I have not been the easiest author to work with: once the window of time I had set aside for completion of the work was exceeded, it was difficult to keep to a schedule. People who publish books must have the patience of Job, the determination of Sisyphus, the grit of McAdam, and the gentility of Miss Manners. My hat is off to them.

Michael J. Lewis
University of California, Davis
December 1995

1

Introduction

I don't really remember a time when I didn't know about stout. My earliest and most formative years, the late thirties and early forties, were spent in Wales in the Rhondda Valley among my noisy and extended family of miners. Cutting coal, playing rugby, choral singing, and beer drinking were inextricably and logically linked activities that more or less occupied my family's entire life. As in most tribal societies, my family was a matriarchy governed by my grandmother and her sister, Great Aunt Sophie, who broke into English only when instructions shouted loudly in Welsh failed to produce results. Grandmother and Great Aunt Sophie dressed always in black; they were ladies one could not easily put one's arms around. They were also stout drinkers: not by choice, you understand, but for medicinal reasons — same as the snuff. Thus, I came early to appreciate the calming and healthful effects of a good glass of stout. I wish I could recall mam-gu giving me a taste of this potion, for I could now celebrate and justify my lifelong delight and even addiction to stouts by that. However, I think grandmother would have regarded that as a waste.

My grandfather and uncles all worked in the coal pits, coming home every evening in blackface with staring white eyes and ruby mouths and smelling of coal dust and damp. They would strip off and bathe one after the other in a huge tin tub before the roaring coal fire, leaving behind bath water the color of Guinness. Then they would eat and vanish "down the club" most nights for beer. What a wonder it was to lie snug in bed on warm weekend evenings and listen to a dozen or more slightly tipsy Welsh miners — victorious from rugby and full of beer — singing below my bedroom window that overlooked the only lamppost on Meyler Street. They sang with feeling those folk songs that glorify the language and celebrate the country and the people, and so define the heart of Welsh culture. But they were not tipsy on stout. Only my uncles and others who had been to England, London even, would dare to enjoy in public the healthful draught of stout old ladies that came in bottles.

The first time I ever remember drinking much stout was in its guise of a healing, nutritious, and strengthening drink. Guinness, of course, had long ago advertised: "Guinness for Strength: Think What Toucan Do." The ad had a picture of a large bird with a multi-colored bill. I never really understood that ad.

One hot summer (a rare enough occasion in Wales that I dare say I could put a date on it if necessary by looking at the meteorological records for the Vale of Glamorgan) I had a heavy lifting job which wearied my bones and muscles. Every lunchtime I enjoyed a Mackeson stout to wash down y bara caws (the bread and cheese). It seemed to me the work in the afternoons passed much more easily than in the mornings, and I've been an advocate of a pint at lunchtime ever since.

Sometime earlier than this, however, was when I consumed my first official beer. It was bought for me by my dear late father who was not himself a drinking man, being chapel and later church. He would drink only a light ale once in a while to lay the dust in his mellifluous evensong baritone throat. For what he assumed was my first introduction to beer (I think I was fourteen or fifteen), he chose bottled Guinness on the general theory that a sufficiently distasteful experience would turn me off beer for good. Wrong. I had been in the habit of slipping down to the Journey's End or the Gipsy's Tent for a half of bitter for a year or more. In fact, I think I was more familiar with the pleasures of beers and pubs than he. Ironically, I had also been smoking Woodbines for years when he tried to turn me off tobacco with a cigar. I've loved both cigars and stouts ever since, and often at the same time.

In 1971 I went on leave from the University of California to the British School of Malting and Brewing, arriving there about the time Dr. Thomas Young joined the faculty. We became good friends and have remained so ever since. Our friendship was cemented over endless lunchtime pints of Guinness that we purchased and consumed in a wretched/lovely (if you know what I mean) old Victorian city pub. It was at the bottom of the hill from the university near the Ariel Motorcycle Works, now closed, and between the best fish-and-chip shop in Birmingham and the Jalna Indian Restaurant. Tom and I retired there every lunchtime for two or four (you buy me one — I'll buy you one) pints of Guinness with fish and chips and blazing pipefuls of St. Bruno flake shag. When we were joined by the late Professor Jim Hough, a great man and a dear friend, we ate at the Jalna or over at the Hare and Hounds, which was the nearest draught Bass to the university. Lunches were memorable and were never wasted on sandwiches and reading. Yet these lunches had such extraordinary effects on my waistline that it was a considerable time after my return to California that I managed to shed the excess avoirdupois so diligently gained.

I am fortunate enough to get back to Britain most years, sometimes even twice. During these trips I visit breweries and have recently had the good fortune to visit Guinness Park Royal (London) and Dublin and Young's in Wandsworth, and to drink the stouts in those breweries in the company of the brewers who made them. In Britain it is my habit to go down the length of the bar taps half-pint at a time, usually from left to right, to explore the flavors available. After that excursion (if still able) I revert to stout drinking, whether Guinness or Beamish or Murphy's or the breweries' own stout products, now much more commonly available than formerly.

So stout is my tipple, and when asked what are my favorite beers, Guinness is at the top of the list along with Budweiser (odd, you may say, but true), then come Worthington White Shield, Sierra Nevada Pale Ale, and almost any single malt scotch.

No other beer style in the world more closely embodies the ideas of quality, value, and flavor than does stout. What stronger representation of image and value is there than a thick, creamy, black pint of Guinness doing the nitrogen roll to perfection right out of the tap, then served with a four-leaf clover outlined in the ivory-colored foam? I recently enjoyed such a pint of Guinness with my son in a crowded bar in Cape Town, South Africa. In a pub (and indeed a country) where almost all the beer consumed is of the light lager style, we certainly made our statement.

4

Stout is a wonderful beverage that has been enjoyed for some 250 years by Irishmen, Englishmen, soldiers, mothers, and monks alike. Perhaps no other beverage in the world has such a calming way and the universal ability to warm on a cool night, refresh on a hot afternoon, and heal a wounded soul. For these reasons I believe the future of stout is quite good.

When Elizabeth Gold, the publisher at Brewers Publications, asked me whom I could recommend to write this stout book, I volunteered myself. Given a second chance, I might have voted differently: however, after looking back over what I've written, I think I've paid my dues. As I complete this opening chapter, I look forward to the adventure to follow, and I hope you enjoy it with me.

2

The Origin of Stouts

As far as I can tell, the earliest use of the word "stout" clearly referring to a beer beverage appears in a letter of 1677 in the Egerton Manuscript now in a British museum. It reads: "We will drink to your health both in stout and best wine." This implies to me some equivalency between these two beverages and hence the excellence of stout. In the same vein, in his *Journal to Stella*, Jonathan Swift (an Irish-born man of letters and a clergyman, who should perhaps know his stout) writes:

Or kindly when his credit's out
Surprise him with a pint of stout

In 1734 *The London and Country Brewer*, an anonymous text, first appeared and went on to run many editions over the next twenty-five years. In this publication, "stout butt beer" is mentioned as a feature of London breweries of those times. Redman[1] points out that "entire butt beer" was the brewers' description of porter at the time. He assumes, however, that stout butt beer is merely stronger or an export porter and is not a true stout. In his commentary on these passages, Corran[2] insists that at this time stout was nothing like today's black beers we call stouts. Part of the evidence is that Faulkner, in 1741, comments, "Stout; a cant word for strong *beer*" (my emphasis). What an odd thing to say if stout merely meant strong, a view Redman[1] supports. I am quite sure that *all* beers at the dawn of the eighteenth century were unlike those today, which is probably a good thing, too. But are we too quick to dismiss these few references to stout as meaning merely, as Corran[2] suggests, "any strong brown beer"? Was there in fact at the end of the seventeenth century, and the early part of the eighteenth, a product that could reasonably have been a black beer stout?

First, of course, the authors of these works, including Swift, had as many words available to them meaning "strong" as we do today. Why then choose by accident the word stout if it were not clearly informative to the reader?

Second, the idea that stouts were not black beers, as today, again begs the question, Who says so? The implication is that such beers were somehow impossible. But this cannot be. Although machines for roasting coffee and grain were not yet invented, coffee roasting and coffee houses were common at the time, and indeed coffee was in danger of replacing ale as the preferred drink of the intelligentsia, even as it is today with all those fancy coffees available!

Coffee roasting and grain roasting are exactly parallel technologies and it wouldn't surprise me if some clever brewer hadn't thought to compete with coffee by using roasted grains. Roasted grain as a potential adulterant of coffee and a substitute for coffee (for example, with chicory essence) has long been popular in Britain and a base for a hot beverage elsewhere. Certainly beers at that time were made with high quantities of dried brown malts, well on their way to being black; some early porters were even flavored with *burnt* molasses.[1] So it is possible that stouts existed in the late seventeenth century and were sufficiently common to enter the contemporary literature. Whether you agree or not, my argument, I think, has as much to commend it as the argument which insists the word "stout" in these references means simply "strong beer." I've argued the case for porter arising from stout, which is quite the contrary to most histories; porter began to appear some years after these references. This is, after all, a stout book and the history of beer is murky enough to have it come out the way this author prefers! In fact, even Redman[1] refers to an 1805 description of strong London porter as being "better known as Brown Stout."

A recitation by Obadiah Poundage, quoted in Corran's *The Origin of Porter*,[3] implies that at the end of the seventeenth century, as a result of wars with France, the tax on malt (and on the coal and coke used to process it) increased substantially. Hops were much less taxed. This caused brewers to use less malt and to increase the hops in beers — a strategy that would hardly be used today! Apparently, at that time ales were not, or not very much, hopped. As a result customers began to blend cheaper, lower-gravity but heavily hopped beers with expensive, sweet, high-gravity but lightly hopped ales in the pubs to meet their preferences. (There is a reference often to a third ingredient of stale beer, or twopenny, in a "three threads" [three-thirds] drink, but it is not at all clear what that means. Obadiah suggests some wealthy householders invested in the staling of beer for this purpose! How odd. Could it have been a souring to add some edge to the still sweet ale-beer mixture?)

Obadiah laments, "Our tastes but slowly alter or reform." That is, despite the efforts of brewers, the customers tried to create the drinks they were used to. So the story goes of Ralph Harwood of the Bell Brewery, Shoreditch, London, who brewed a beer to replace these mixtures. His beer was called "Entire" or "Entire Butt," which evolved into porter, named for the workers and working classes who drank it. Alternatively, the name might have originated from the cry "Porter!" intended to clear the way of those delivering the casks of Harwood's beer,[1] though that is not the report of contemporaries. Who knows! Obadiah reports that during his lifetime in brewing, the quality of porter improved beyond any expectation, especially with regard to clarity, resulting from "better workmanship, better malt, better hops, and the use of isinglass."[3]

The first reference to porter is in a letter home by a M. Cesar de Saussure who, after marveling at the extraordinary consumption of beer even among the poor of London "who do not know what it is to quench their thirst with water" (despite the fairly good quality of it), comments that porter, so called because it is drunk by the working classes, is "a thick and strong beverage" that, at three pence the pot, "drunk in excess has the same effect as wine." I write about porter at this stage because stouts are normally assumed to have arisen from porters and to have derived their name and characteristic color and flavor from "stout porter," presumably a stronger and perhaps darker version of ordinary porters. Porter, because of its alcoholic strength and high hop rate, was a very stable beer, certainly by the standard of the times, and could be stored to build up stocks and improve flavor. It was therefore the first beer technologically suited to large-scale production. Samuel Whitbread was the most successful eighteenth century porter brewer. The Whitbread Brewing Company brewed a special 250th Anniversary Porter in 1992. After the demise of the porter trade, in which so many great breweries made their mark, including the preeminent names in stout brewing today, most became ale and stout breweries, including Whitbread. Only a few specialized in stout, the most famous, of course, being the great brewery at St. James's Gate, Dublin, Ireland.

At least from about 1670 right after the public brewers were incorporated as a Guild and very likely even earlier, there was a brewery at St. James's Gate in Dublin.[4] One of the gates to the city, its name came from a parish in that locality extending back at least to the twelfth century. Being on a good supply of water and close to the grain growing regions of central Ireland, it was a favored spot for breweries. Robert Letters (personal communications) advises that in 1759 the water supply to the brewery at St. James's Gate was derived from the Dodder and Poddle Rivers, which also supplied Dublin. This supply was connected to the Grand Canal in 1776, and the brewing water became known as canal water. An arrangement with the Dublin Corporation in 1850 assured that the brewery was supplied with Grand Canal water only. This water was regarded as excellent for brewing because of its calcium and magnesium bicarbonate content. The main source of canal water was St. James's Well in County Kildare, not at the brewery. Wells were later sunk at the brewery to alleviate water shortages for washing and cooling. Canal water is no longer used for brewing, having been replaced since the 1980s by water from a source in the Wicklow Mountains.

As is true today, some breweries and brewers make better beers than others; the owners of the brewery at St.

James's Gate, the Mee family and later the Rainsford family, made beer that was "thin, weak, musty, and stale and worse than anything except the Ale."[10]

With such a reputation it is hardly surprising they leased the brewery to one Captain Paul Espinasse in 1715. Had Espinasse not fallen from his horse to his death at Drogheda in 1750, we might be enjoying a pint of Espinasse these days; after his death, however, his ale and beer brewery fell into disuse and disrepair; it was this brewery that was leased to Arthur Guinness.

In 1759 Arthur Guinness, at the age of thirty-four and with only three or four years' experience in brewing (in 1773 he claimed to have been brewing for "seventeen or eighteen years") traveled to Dublin with a £100 inheritance in his pocket. Who knows what possessed him, in the middle of the eighteenth century in a turbulent Irish beer market already affected by the importation of cheaper London porter, to invest nearly half this sum in the annual rent of a broken-down brewery at St. James's Gate? He certainly had confidence in the future because he signed a nine-thousand-year lease on the property (perhaps as a joke since the property was advertised to let "for any term of years") and started brewing traditional ales and table beers of the times. Around the 1750s, porter began to enter the Irish market from London at a protected price, paying less than one-sixth the tax of the Irish-brewed beers, which at the time were probably brown ales; brown malt was, after all, less heavily taxed than pale. (The tax man hath much to answer for in the history of humankind!) This made it very difficult for the Irish brewers to compete. Arthur Guinness, nevertheless, persevered and began to produce his Guinness Extra Strong Porter, which within ten years he was exporting to London. During this period of difficult

Figure 2.1. A Guinness drayman with his summer headgear poses with a Percheron (a French breed) around 1910. *Photograph courtesy of Guinness.*

trading, Arthur did in fact seek a brewery in Caernarfon or Holyhead in Wales in order to compete effectively (foreshadowing today's global market). If he had succeeded, we might today refer to Caernarfon Welsh Stout (cwrw du Cymreig — Welsh black beer) as the standard of the world. As a Welshman I wouldn't mind a bit!

From Arthur Guinness's rather small beginnings great things grew — the whole world of stout and the leading stout brewery. Around 1777 the inequitable Excise Duty was relieved and the export of London porter to Ireland decreased dramatically. By 1799 Arthur's brewery was producing only porter, some of which was exported. Guinness always was an exporting company, partly perhaps because beer was not the first beverage sought by Irish folk in the mid-1770s, whiskey and gin being the most popular drinks (as perhaps they were in the famous gin-shops of London, too). The first export of six barrels of Guinness to London left Dublin in 1769, but when Arthur died in 1803 there were already records of sales to the Caribbean of Guinness West Indies Porter. These sales to the Caribbean are probably the origin of Guinness's famous Foreign Extra Stout — undoubtedly made to great strength in order to withstand crossing the Atlantic by ship. Incidentally, the company continued to make porter, sold mostly in Ireland, until 1974 when the porter was discontinued. Nevertheless this first

Figure 2.2. The Guinness brewery in Dublin was the biggest in the world when the engraving above was made, in about 1890. The size of the mash tuns and their mechanical operation bear witness to the sophistication of the brewery at that time. *Photograph courtesy of Guinness.*

trickle of exported beer eventually became a torrent, necessitating barges and ships and the opening of a brewery in London in 1936 (Park Royal).

Upon Arthur's death, three of his sons took over the prospering business, and by the end of the nineteenth century Guinness was enjoyed in places as far apart as America, Africa, and Australia. The popularity of the rather curious black stout we all know and love is such that it is now brewed in forty-six countries and sold in approximately 130! Guinness claims to be the only brewer whose core product is a black beer. Members of the Guinness family are no longer associated with the management of the company.

Of course there are other stout brewers in Ireland, including Beamish (Beamish and Crawford), established as the Cork Porter Brewery in 1792,[16] and Murphy's in Cork — both producing rather dry stouts. The Beamish and Crawford and Murphy's breweries are each located in the Irish city of Cork, which is situated in the green hills of the southwestern shores of Ireland on the River Lee. Cork has a rich tradition of brewing, as the malted barley from the nearby limestone fields make wonderful raw materials for stout, and the pure water from the city's wells seems to hold miraculous properties for brewers and Christians alike. In fact, Lady's Well, where the Murphy's brewery was founded in 1856, was dedicated to the Virgin Mary herself, and every year in May pilgrims from around Ireland and the world make their way to Cork to give homage to the miraculous powers of this celebrated well.[17]

During the late eighteenth century, the city and county of Cork had a combined population of only about eighty thousand persons, but as many as nineteen small retail breweries (brewpubs) and twenty-five commercial breweries operated in 1770. Perhaps from this local brewing tradition sprang the stout style. However, from at least one man's perspective, the quality of beer in Cork was poor: "The beer is by far the worst I have ever tasted" (William Doyt, 1785). Not surprisingly, during this time, the more technically advanced ales from English breweries were finding a large market in Cork. For example, in 1788, over sixty thousand barrels were being brought into the Cork port from England.[16]

The breweries of Cork have a long history of consolidation and buyout, starting in the 1790s. All but one of the retail breweries went out of operation or were purchased by 1791, and of the forty-four breweries in operation in 1770, only thirty remained by 1795. But the Cork breweries began to adopt the more advanced British brewing techniques, and by the end of the century almost all of the ale importations from England had stopped. The industry continued concentrating, and by 1805, only nine breweries were producing beer in Cork.[18]

The remaining breweries of Cork thrived during the 1800s in an agricultural environment ideal for growing barley, including the soft water from the River Lee, well suited for brewing beer. Specifically, the fields surrounding Cork have a relatively high concentration of limestone, which both alkalizes the soil and provides calcium and magnesium for the growing barley plant. This, along with the relatively temperate climate and predictable rainfall of southern Ireland, makes the region excellent for barley cultivation.[19]

In addition, the breweries of Cork were aided by several excise tax duties, both Irish and English, that favored the consumption of local beer over whiskey or imported beer. Similarly, and probably most importantly,

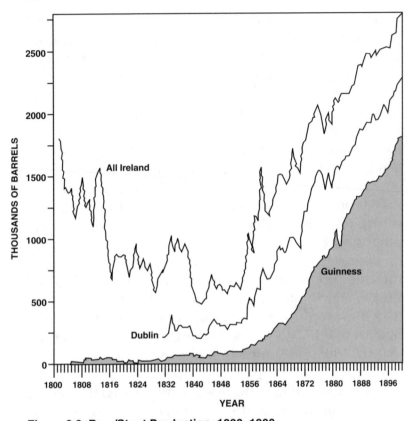

Figure 2.3. Beer/Stout Production, 1800–1900
Source: Information taken from Raymond Crotty, *Ireland in Crisis: A Study in Capitalistic Colonial Underdevelopment* (Dingle County, Kerry, Ireland: Brandon Book Publishers): 50.

the great Irish famine of the 1840s caused tremendous despair among the population. As sad as that was, it benefitted the brewers, the local producers of cheap beer in a society where many were seeking oblivion in alcohol. Brewers enjoyed a very advantageous business position during that time.

As the breweries in Cork thrived under this huge local demand, the taste for stout in England began to grow, and Guinness began its fabulous rise to domination of the stout market in England. In 1833, Guinness passed the Cork brewery of Beamish and Crawford as the largest brewer in Ireland.[18] In 1837, however, Dublin accounted for only 30 percent of all the beer produced in Ireland; most of the remaining 70 percent was produced by the various breweries in Cork (figure 2.3).[19]

After 1844, the total output of the breweries in Cork increased fairly continuously, as evidenced by the total amount of tax-paid malt.[8] In 1848, 135,828 bushels of malt were used by the city brewers. Fifty years later, the number had more than quadrupled to 563,704.[16]

Beamish and Crawford and James A. Murphy's have been cross-town rivals since the Murphy brothers started brewing in 1856. Beamish, however, is clearly the older of the two, founded initially as a partnership between William Beamish, William Crawford, both local merchants, and brewers Richard Barrett and Digby O'Brien in 1792.[16] This partnership rented a brewery on South Main Street in Cork (a part of the current brewery) from an Edward Allen. Founded by his father, Aylmer Allen, who had been brewing there since 1715, Allen's brewery was then the largest in Cork. There is evidence that a brewery had been on site since 1600.[17]

When O'Brien died in 1795 and Barrett retired from the beer business in 1800, the families of Beamish and Crawford came into complete control of the company and remained in control until the late nineteenth century. With new control of the brewery William Beamish and William Crawford hired a number of men from London who were skilled in the advanced British brewing techniques. These men were instrumental in implementing the latest brewing technology, and their fabulous chocolatey dry stout produced on South Main Street increased

sales for the brewery. By 1800 Beamish and Crawford
was the largest brewer in Ireland, a position it enjoyed
until 1833.[16]

One of the contributing factors to Beamish and
Crawford's success was their near total vertical integra-
tion. As noted earlier, the area surrounding Cork is ideal
for the production of barley, and in the early 1800s there
were over twenty-five maltsters in Cork. Many of these
supplied the distilleries of Ireland, but Beamish and
Crawford owned six malting houses that supplied solely
the breweries of the area. Because of this they achieved
massive economies of scale and market advantage over
the other, smaller brewers. In addition, Beamish and
Crawford also controlled real estate in and around Cork,
some flour-mills, and, of course, the many tied house
pubs. At the peak of their market dominance, Beamish
and Crawford had invested over £250,000 in their various properties; by 1860 the brewery itself covered over
five acres of prime, inner city real estate.[20]

Little is known about the Beamish and Crawford
brewery design before 1865, but one report states that
there were "eighteen large vats in 1850." Brewery power
came from two, twenty-horsepower steam engines,
which had taken over from the horse-driven mills before
1819. Between 1818 and 1861, brewery upgrades were
constantly made, evidenced by the fact that output
increased by 150 percent while the number employed
had fallen from 500 to 360. In 1865, the brewery was
entirely rebuilt at a cost of £100,000; this included four
coppers (kettles), each of 1,560-gallon content (fifty barrels); new refrigerators; large pumps; and fermenters.
Two new thirty-five- and forty-five-horsepower steam
engines had been installed, and Beamish and Crawford
had brought in-house all engineering, smithing, and

coopering.[20] The investment in this brewery paid off: production rose from 96,000 barrels in 1885 to over 130,000 barrels by the turn of the century.[19]

Like all the Cork breweries, Beamish and Crawford also has a long history of brewery buyout and consolidation. First, in 1901, it acquired the Southgate Brewery, founded in 1758 and possibly the oldest brewery in Ireland still operating at the time.[17] Then, just five years later, St. Stephens brewery was bought outright, and in 1914 Beamish and Crawford bought the Bandon Brewing Company, also of Cork. In turn, Beamish was bought out by Canadian Breweries (later Carling O'Keefe) in 1962. This buyout led to a brewery modernization and the brewing of Carling Black Label at the Beamish breweries in 1964.

In 1987, Elders IXL of Australia, then the fourth largest brewer in the world, acquired Carling O'Keefe, which led to the introduction of Foster's lager into the Irish market. Elders IXL, at the same time, bought Britain's Courage, and now the Beamish Irish Stout is available throughout England through the tied house pubs controlled by Courage.[17]

The younger of the two major Cork breweries was founded in 1856 at the famous Lady's Well by four brothers: James, William, Jerome, and Francis Murphy.[16] Initially, they brewed porter, but switched to stout to emulate the popular style of the time. Most of the water used by the brewery came from the well, and the local bishop's regular blessing of the well undoubtedly helped the Murphy brothers brew good stout.

The Murphy brothers had excellent timing; when they burst onto the scene in 1856, demand for stout was increasing dramatically. Continuing a Cork tradition, Murphy's acquired a number of tied houses all over southern Ireland to expand its market. In 1859 Righard Pigot Beamish commented:

> Our opponents the Murphy's have succeeded in establishing a sale of some 40,000 tierces [about 54,000 barrels] and have steadily captured one-third of our town customers. They are now proceeding to attack us in the country district, and the result of the battle may be the necessity of a large expenditure of money, of course greatly reducing the net profits.[21]

Murphy's continued to expand by acquiring other breweries. In 1901, Murphy's bought Arnotts Brewery and Riverstown Ale brewery, and promptly closed each of them down. This provided Murphy's with additional tied houses in Cork, which was the basis of the company's growth.[16] They also developed an export trade, mainly to the English West Midlands.

Behind these aggressive tactics, Murphy's is now the number two brewer in Ireland. James Murphy and Company signed a licensing agreement with Heineken in 1975. This sparked tremendous investment in new equipment, and now Murphy's boasts one of the most modern breweries in all of Ireland. Keeping the relation with the church alive, the new brewery was blessed by the local bishop, and witnessed by the prime minister of the Republic of Ireland (figure 2.4). In 1983, Murphy's was bought out completely by Heineken, and now Murphy's is sold around the world using Heineken's vast marketing power and expertise.[17]

Recently, Murphy's has become available in American supermarkets in a tall, sixteen-ounce can, replicating technology used by Guinness. The "Genuine Pub Draught" technology provides the nitrogen "rolling" effect of tradi-

Figure 2.4. The new Murphy's brewery in Cork is blessed by the local bishop in 1985. *Photograph by Michael Jackson, from* The New World Guide to Beer, *180. Reprinted by permission.*

tional pub-style dispense. The stout is wonderfully dry and drinkable. Although most Americans have seen or indeed have imbibed a pint or a can of Guinness, few have even heard of Murphy's. But the combination of dispensing technology and of fantastic stout may soon make inroads to the burgeoning stout market in the United States.

21

Figure 2.5.
The Uxbridge Arms in Notting Hill, London, has been a Whitbread Pub for over a hundred years. *Reprinted by permission from Whitbread from An* Uncommon Brewer: The Story of Whitbread, 1742–1992, *103.*

STOUT BREWING IN ENGLAND

Although I earlier argued the case for stout preceding porter, there is clear evidence that commercial brewing of stout in England grew out of the wide popularity of porter in London and elsewhere. The ever increasing importation of Guinness to the English market during the mid- to late nineteenth century surely drove many English brewers to emulate the Irish style. For the most part, however, the stouts made in England and Scotland during this time were not dry like Irish stout but sweet, many containing portions of milk sugar.

Whitbread, one of the larger breweries of the late nineteenth century, first brewed Mackeson Milk Stout in 1907 at their brewery in Hythe, Kent, and more recently in Samlesbury, Lancashire. The brewery subsequently abandoned its porter style and has advertised itself as "Whitbread's Ale and Stout" (figure 2.5). It is rumored that farmers in Kent had asked for the right for their cows to pass through the brewery grounds, contributing to the idea of a "milk" product.

Many other breweries in England also have records of brewing stout. Anchor Brewery (one of many worldwide who share this name) of South London has records of a "Russian Stout" being exported to the Baltic as early as the 1780s, with specific gravity of over 1.100![22] This style reportedly used the same conditioning method while in transit as the famous India pale ale. Many breweries in England and Scotland still produce stout, but it is clearly a secondary style for British brewers. However, it is uncommon to frequent a British pub and find it devoid of a tap dedicated to stout. Guinness, on the strength of its Park Royal Brewery, dominates the British stout market, but many other breweries produce a similar drink for regional and local consumption (see accompanying map, figure 2.6).

There are numerous long-standing traditions about stouts in which Guinness played a part — as might be expected from the fact it is the most ubiquitous of the stout products. The nutritional and even healing value of stouts are among its enduring qualities and have been often advertised, although it is likely the advertising followed, rather than led, the public's perceptions in this matter. There is a famous quotation[4] from an Irish Dragoon wounded at the Battle of Waterloo in 1815 who wrote home from Belgium:

> When I was sufficiently recovered to be permitted nourishment I felt an extraordinary desire for a glass of Guinness which I knew could be obtained without difficulty. I am confident that it contributed more than anything else to my recovery.

Figure 2.6. Map of the Historical Development of Stout

Ireland
- Guinness, St. James's Gate, Dublin. Established 1759. Water supply: Wicklow Mountains.

- James A. Murphy's Ltd., Cork, Ireland. Established 1856. Water supply: Lady's Well, Cork.

- Beamish and Crawford, Cork, Ireland. Established 1792. Water supply: River Cork.

Yorkshire
- John Smith's Tadcaster Brewery, Tadcaster, North Yorkshire. Established 1758.

- Samuel Smith Ole Brewery, Tadcaster, North Yorkshire. Established 1758.

Central England
- Burton Bridge Brewery, Burton upon Trent, Staffordshire. Established 1846. Water supply: Artesian Wells of Burton.

- Hoskins & Oldfield, North Mills, Frog Island, Leicster. Established 1877.

Eastern England
- Banks and Taylor Brewing Ltd., Shefford, Bedfordshire. Established 1884.

- Maudons Brewery, Sudbury, Suffolk. Established 1793.

London
- Park Royal Brewery (Guinness) London. Established 1936. Water supply: Thames River.

- Young's & Company, Wandsworth (near London). Established 1675.

Northwest
- Whitbread's Brewing Company, Samlesbury, Lancashire. Established 1669.

Guinness was also available in the Crimean War — Florence Nightingale eat your heart out! In fact stouts have had a long tradition of possessing useful nutritive value, of giving strength, and of being used as a tonic. Stouts have been praised by medical professionals in bygone years, as contributing to alleviating all sorts of

My Goodness
My Christmas
GUINNESS

Figure 2.7. Contemporary Guinness Christmas card.

ailments — including insomnia, debility ("as a natural tonic I think it has few equals"), neurasthenia, constipation ("dispense with the usual artificial bowel stimulation"), and digestion ("the finest tonic we possess"). Furthermore, for nursing mothers stout or other beer is a tradition of great antiquity. Henry Grattan in 1782 wrote to Guinness that brewers were "the actual nurse of the people and entitled to every encouragement and favor and exemption."[4]

Michael Jackson[5] reports that the British advertising agency S. H. Benson asked drinkers in 1920 why they favored Guinness. A common response was, "It does me good." This probably confirmed an ingrained view of stouts as a tonic and was the source of a long and successful program of advertising, including the immortal "Guinness Is Good for You" and later "My Goodness, My Guinness," and of course "Guinness for Strength."

In 1909 Guinness was taken on a expedition to the South Pole — for its medicinal value, no doubt. Some eighteen years later the abandoned base camp was uncovered. According to Australian explorer Douglas Mawson the four bottles of Guinness found, "although frozen, were put to excellent use."[10]

Milk and cream stouts arose perhaps as a means of boosting the already implied healthful properties of stout by adding milk products such as lactose or whey, or (in one patent) concentrated peptonized (partially hydrolyzed) milk.[6] Remember, adding milk solids to chocolate was a nineteenth-century achievement initially used to improve nutrition. Of course lactose cannot be fermented by brewers' yeasts and so stays in the beer where it might add some residual roundness (although it is not a sweet sugar) and texture to the finished product, as well as calories.

The very sweet and strong Castle Milk Stout of South African Breweries, claims to have "Good Health in Every Glass" — a claim that would hardly survive scrutiny in this country. Anton Piendl[6] examined this claim by comparing this stout to others on the basis of vitamins (especially thiamine) and minerals (especially iron). He found this particular milk stout not to be unusually different from other stouts (table 2.1).

Among the most well-known, lactose-containing milk stouts (probably containing lactose approaching 10 percent of the grist weight) is Mackeson made by Whitbread (established 1669). The export version is undoubtedly stronger than the same beer on the domestic

TABLE 2.1

	Milk Stout[a]	Regular Stout[b]	
Minerals			
Potassium	377.00	597.00	mg/L
Sodium	259.00	18.00	mg/L
Calcium	30.00	32.00	mg/L
Magnesium	99.00	86.00	mg/L
Copper	0.22	0.23	mg/L
Iron	0.20	0.23	mg/L
Manganese	0.18	0.22	mg/L
Zinc	0.06	0.07	mg/L
Vitamins			
Thiamine	9	26	μg/L
Riboflavin	237	453	μg/L
Pyridoxine	233	469	μg/L
Pantothenic Acid	439	1,347	μg/L
Niacine	5,233	6,867	μg/L
Biotin	8	13	μg/L

Source: Information taken from Anton Piendl, *Brauindustrie*, no. 4 (1982): 225–231.

Note: There is an unusually high concentration of sodium in the Castle Stout.

[a] Castle Milk Stout
[b] Guinness Extra Stout

British market. Another famous brewer, Bass & Co., was active in the porter and stout trade, although much more famous for pale ales and draught bitter. D. M. Lay, librarian at the Bass Museum (personal communication), advises that the Bass stouts carried a "P" number from P2 Imperial Stout (the strongest and most expensive) to P3 (Extra Stout), Double Stout (P4), and Stout (P5). These stouts enjoyed a high reputation and were exported widely, especially P2. This product was available in the United States from around 1870 to the start of Prohibition. However, in 1917 restrictions on raw materials associated with the First World War caused all but the P2 to be discontinued. Then in 1967, when Bass merged with Charrington, P2 was discontinued in favor of the Charrington products Jubilee Stout and Sweetheart Stout. During its heyday P2, with a specific gravity of 1.098 or about 25 °Plato, fitted right in with the very strong stouts made by other brewers; even the weakest, P5, was brewed close to 1.070 or about 18 °Plato. A peek at the Bass brewing books for 1890 and 1966 shows that P2 declined from an OG of about 1.100 (25 °Plato) to 1.078 (19 °Plato) in these years. (Incidentally, the No. 3 Bass brewery took just about twelve hours to make 260 barrels of P2 from mash-in to

Figure 2.8. The horses of Samuel Smith travel along the main street of Tadcaster. The Angel and White Horse is the brewery tap. *Photograph courtesy of Merchan Du Vin.*

TABLE 2.2

Beers and Ales — German and English Types

	German Lager Beers			English Ale and Stout	
	Vienna	Pilsen	Munich	Bass' Ale	Guinness' Stout
Present Specific Gravity	1.0162	1.0136	1.0203	1.0060	1.0127
Indication by Balling	4.0000	3.4000	5.1000	1.5000	3.1700
Absolute Alcohol (by weight)	3.7500	3.5500	3.8000	6.3900	6.3600
Volatile Acidity (as Acetic Acid)	0.0230	0.0260	0.0090	0.0180	0.0516
Total Unfermented Solid Extract	5.8900	5.1500	6.9300	4.3700	6.0500
Fixed Acidity (as Lactic Acid)	0.1240	0.1300	0.1370	0.2200	0.3700
Fermentable Sugar in Extract (Maltose)	0.1610	0.9200	1.5300	0.9600	1.7500
Albuminoids (Nitrogen x 6.25)	0.7770	0.7660	0.6430	0.5490	7.4500
Ash	0.2170	0.1970	0.2350	0.3180	0.3000
Ratio of Fermentable to Non-Fermentable Matter	1:2.65	1:4.58	1:3.52	1:3.55	1:2.46
Original Gravity of Wort (about) Balling	12.600	11.600	13.800	16.100	17.700
Real Degree of Fermentation	54.700	56.700	51.000	73.500	66.600
Ratio of Alcohol to Extract	1:1.57	1:1.45	1:1.82	1:0.68	1:0.95

Source: Information taken from *Practical Points for Brewers* (New York: National Brewers Academy, 1993).

pitching with yeast and used 600 pounds of hops in the product. The product spent only thirty-five hours in the fermenting squares.)

Oatmeal stouts have enjoyed something of a revival, those from Samuel Smith's (Tadcaster) and Young's (Wandsworth) being widely available in the United States; each contains about 5 percent grist weight of oatmeal. Perhaps this grain was also first used to promote the healthy image of stout, as it is not otherwise a particularly desirable brewing grain. Our own experience with oatmeal as a brewing ingredient suggests a significant contribution of astringency; this is hardly akin to the "silky" character commonly detected in such stouts by beer writers.

The association of stouts with certain kinds of foods has long intrigued gastronomes — especially its association with seafood, particularly oysters. The Irish stout brewers regularly support several oyster festivals. Benjamin Disreali, British prime minister in Victoria's reign, wrote to his sister, following a division in the House of Parliament, "I then left the House and supped at the Carlton with a large party off oysters, Guinness and broiled bones."[4] Some stouts have been made with oyster extract or shells as a useful ingredient, perhaps originally as a fining agent; certainly ground shells were used in ancient times to control excess acidity, probably arising from bacterial contamination.

Porters and stouts pack quite an alcoholic wallop to go along with their extraordinary flavor impact. *Practical Points for Brewers*[7] produced the additional analyses shown in table 2.2 in which the original gravity of Guinness FES was estimated to be 17.7 °Plato. At the same time Bass Ale was shown to be 16.1 °Plato. In contrast the German lager beers recorded (table 2.2) were closer to today's gravity. The same document gives the following general points on porter brewing:

> The water must be soft. The malt must be very high dried. The black color malt must be of good quality. The ratio of sugar to non-sugar should be 1:0.44. The conversion temperature should be 152°F and the resting temperature 160°F.

> Extract to be derived from the malt _____80%
> Extract to be derived from the sugar_____20%
> Black color malt (grist weight) _____10%

Portion of water to malt	6:1 by weight
Amount of sparge water	55% of total water
Temperature of the sparge water	160°F
Hops of fine quality	3.5% on extract
Total yeast	1.25% on extract

All the proceedings of mashing, sparging, boiling, hopping, cooling, yeasting, and fermenting are conducted in exactly the same manner as described for ales.

The Wahl-Henius *American Handy-book of Brewing and Malting*, volume 11,[8] describes stout as "having a very dark color, malt flavor and sweet taste, brewed stronger than ale and possessing a tart taste in the aged product, but less alcohol than ale; usually lively." Porter is "brewed like a stout but not so strong." Analysis of stouts contained in the same book dating from the end of the last century and the beginning of this one show beers of unusual strength (table 2.3) ranging from 15 to 23 °Plato with alcohol contents from 5 percent to over 7 percent by weight. Anton Piendl's data (table 2.4) shows porters and stouts of unusual strength, and we have analyzed a number of modern products, too (see table 5.2 in chapter 5). In this day and age the tradition continues with products like Guinness Foreign Extra Stout and Tuborg's Double Imperial Stout which, for example, is at about 18 °Plato.

In his chapter on porters and stouts, Michael Jackson[5] suggests that brewers who make both porter and stout make the porter less full bodied, though not necessarily less alcoholic than their stout. He suggests that porters and stouts existed longer in London and Dublin because the water in these great cities was less well suited for brewing in the new era of pale dry hopped ales that began to appear by 1830 and contributed to the demise of porter. He further suggests that stouts persisted in Ireland long after their decline in England because Irish maltsters could still roast their grains to high color (restrictions on energy use during the First World War made it difficult for English maltsters to roast grains at an acceptable price, and Redman[1] points to this as the death knell of porter). Finally, Guinness so dominated the Irish national market because of their size, access to the canal system of the island, and their adoption of the O'Neill harp (actually a mirror image of the symbol of the Irish nation) as their trade mark in 1862.

Taxonomy, the classification of things based on their relation to each other, can be made simple or complex depending on whether one is a lumper or splitter. I am a lumper and my tasting experience tells me some stouts are sweet tasting (including some milk, cream, and oatmeal stouts) and others are not (dry stouts). Further classification does not help me much. The imperial sort of stout is based on a long tradition of export to the East (especially Russia) but not on any obvious flavor difference, brewing method, or analytic quality (e.g., unique alcoholic strength, though this was originally and obviously a necessity for such an export trade). *Michael Jackson's Beer Companion*[5] contains a fascinating account of the history of imperial stouts (as well as porters and sweet and dry stouts), and something of Jackson's experiences in visiting those breweries in what used to be called the Eastern Block. He notes, however, that imperial stouts are called porters (table 2.4) in the East when they are made there, which just goes to show there is not much in a name. The following is from Michael's book:

When a high gravity, roasted grains, and often a warm fermentation, perhaps with an ale yeast, are combined, the result is a brew of extraordinary power and complexity. Its intensity calls to mind the tarry sweetness of Pedro Ximenez sherry. The roastiness melds with smoky, tar-like, burnt, fruity, estery notes and alcohol flavors. There is a suggestion of cocoa, or strong coffee on a winter's night. The fruitiness is reminiscent of the burnt currants on the edge of a cake that has just been removed from the oven, or the Christmas pudding traditional in Britain, heavy with dried and candied fruits. The alcohol suggests that the cocoa or coffee, pudding or cake has been laced with spirit.

I love stouts with the best of them but I could never write that!

Closer to home, Roger Bergen,[9] in *A Stout Companion*, has also expressed his personal opinions and descriptions of the stouts available in Britain, elsewhere in the world, and in this country.

TABLE 2.3A

	Lbs. Hops in Kettle, Per Quarter Malt (336 Lbs.)	Gravity Long	Hops in Kettle Per American Barrel	Balling of Wort
London pale bitter ale	8–10 lbs.	20–21	1½–2 lbs.	14
Burton mild ale	7–8 lbs.	19–21	1¼–1¾ lbs.	14
London four ale (mild)	4–7 lbs.	19–21	1–1¼ lbs.	13–14
Burton strong ale	10–14 lbs.	23–25	2–3 lbs.	16–17
Burton pale ale	12–15 lbs.	23–25	2½–3 lbs.	16–17
Burton export ale	18–20 lbs.	25–27	3½–4 lbs.	17–18
Porter	4–8 lbs.	18–22	1– ½ lbs.	13–15
Single stout	8–10 lbs.	23–27	1½–2 lbs.	16–18
Double stout	10–12 lbs.	27–30	2–2½ lbs.	18–20
Imperial stout	14–15 lbs.	30–40	2½–3 lbs.	20–25
Russian export	16 lbs.	above 40	3¼ lbs.	above 25

TABLE 2.3B

Ales, Porters, Stouts, American Weissbeers, and Special Beers	Time of Analysis	Balling of Beer	Balling of Wort	Water	Alcohol by Wt.	Real Extract	Album-inoids	Sugar	Lactic Acid	Ash	Phosphoric Acid	Analyzed By	Obtained In
Stouts													
Guinness' Extra													
Bottled Foreign Stout	1901	3.40	18.22	87.56	6.29	6.15	0.75	0.97	0.243	—	0.108	—	Chicago
Guinness' Extra Stout	1896	4.50	17.60	—	5.64	7.02	—	1.03	—	—	—	Doemens	Munich
Allsopp Luncheon Stout	1896	2.97	15.58	—	5.35	5.37	—	1.53	—	—	—	Doemens	Munich
Victoria Stout	1888	2.35	15.62	89.68	5.36	4.90	—	1.30	0.056	acetic acid	—	Doemens	Munich
Dublin Single Stout	1879	6.10	15.18	89.74	4.92	5.34	0.43	—	0.222	acetic acid	0.115	C. Gottfried & C. Rach	Munich
Dublin Double Stout	1879	2.90	20.63	86.60	7.23	6.17	0.78	—	0.364	acetic acid	0.173	Lawrence & Reilly	Munich
Double Brown Stout													
(Barklay, Perkins & Co.)	1884	4.00	18.78	87.28	6.00	6.78	—	—	0.460	0.39	—	V. Fodor	Budapest
Dublin Stout	1882	7.20	23.08	83.66	6.78	9.52	0.43	5.35	0.252	—	—	Ch. Graham	
English Stout	1887	3.70	18.16	87.57	6.13	5.90	0.76	0.57	0.151	0.37	0.049	C. A. Crampton	Wash., USA
American Brown Stout	1900	5.45	18.15	—	5.37	7.83	0.56	2.00	—	—	—	Wahl-Henius Inst.	Chicago
Porters													
American Porter	1887	6.70	17.97	86.32	4.80	8.19	0.76	2.67	0.166	0.41	0.100	C. A. Crampton	Wash., USA
American Porter	1899	2.95	13.25	—	4.19	4.87	0.40	1.49	0.135	—	0.061	Wahl-Henius Inst.	Chicago
Canadian Porter	1900	4.00	14.36	—	4.37	5.91	0.53	1.31	0.162	—	—	Wahl-Henius Inst.	Chicago
Swedish Porter	1907	6.73	19.10	—	5.06	8.98	0.66	2.26	0.144	—	0.115	Wahl-Henius Inst.	Gothenborg, Sweden

Source: Information taken from Robert Wahl and Max Henius, *American Handy-book of Malting and Brewing*, vol. 11 (Chicago: Wahl-Henius Institute, 1908).

TABLE 2.4

Brand Name	Albani Porter	Ceres Porter	Porter Okocimski
Name of the Brewery	Albani Bryggerierne A/S	Ceres Bryggerierne	Okocim Brewery
Place of the Brewery	Odense	Aarhus	Warschau
Country	Denmark	Denmark	Polen
No.	21.00	22.00	23.00
Extract of the Original Wort (°)	19.60	18.50	21.90
Alcohol	5.35	6.37	5.75
Real Extract	9.62	6.64	11.31
Water Content	850.30	869.90	829.40
Caloric Content			
Kilocalories	750.00	701.00	845.00
Kilojoules (kcal x 4.184)	3,138.00	2,934.00	3,536.00
Protein			
Raw Protein (Sol. N x 6.25)	8.40	5.80	11.90
Free Amino Nitrogen (TNBS)	141.00	136.00	328.00
Proline	601.00	402.00	760.00
Minerals			
Potassium	793.00	468.00	1,000.00
Sodium	119.00	33.00	46.00
Calcium	69.00	29.00	55.00
Magnesium	152.00	79.00	218.00
Total Phosphorus	395.00	227.00	610.00
Sulphate	330.00	130.00	267.00
Chloride	440.00	250.00	342.00
Silicate	n.b.	n.b.	n.b.
Nitrate	16.00	8.00	32.00
Copper	0.10	0.01	0.13
Iron	0.04	0.18	3.17
Manganese	0.37	0.13	0.72
Zinc	0.01	0.08	0.03
Vitamins			
Thiamine	48.00	122.00	78.00
Riboflavin	447.00	470.00	855.00
Pyridoxine	1,025.00	450.00	1,075.00
Pantothenic Acid	1,930.00	1,460.00	2,660.00
Niacine	12,560.00	6,867.00	13,300.00
Biotin	30.00	9.00	20.00
Organic Acids			
Pyruvate	94.00	128.00	131.00
Citrate	297.00	187.00	280.00
Malate	115.00	9.00	150.00
L-Lactate	16.00	23.00	570.00
D-Lactate	41.00	44.00	107.00
Acetate	176.00	219.00	185.00
Gluconate	78.00	3.00	4.00
Total Polyphenols	394.00	199.00	485.00
Anthocyanogens	105.00	67.00	194.00
Bitterness	39.50	41.50	26.50
Dissolved Carbon Dioxide	0.53	0.51	0.32
Fermentation By-Products			
Glycerol	1,792.00	2,037.00	1,640.00
n-Propyl Alcohol	15.30	14.10	20.40
i-Butyl Alcohol	22.70	14.20	21.10
i-Amyl Alcohols	72.40	89.20	105.90
2-Phenyl Ethanol	29.40	39.60	16.40
Ethyl Acetate	24.60	38.70	20.20
i-Amyl Acetate	0.60	3.00	1.90
Acetaldehyde	4.50	17.60	10.20
Diacetyl	0.08	0.05	0.05
2.3-Pentanedione	0.04	0.01	0.01
Total Sulphur Dioxide	4.00	17.00	1.00
Hydrogen Ion Concentration	4.49	4.41	4.16
Viscosity	2.87	2.20	2.73
Apparent Degree of Fermentation	64.90	80.70	62.10
Attenuation Limit, apparent	70.10	87.00	66.70
Color	250.00	170.00	248.00

Source: Information taken from Anton Piendl, *Brauindustrie*, no. 4. (1982): 225–31.

TABLE 2.4 (continued)

Tsingtao Porter	Guinness Extra Stout	Foreign Extra Stout Malaysia	Tuborg Imperial Double Stout	
Tsingtao-brauerei	A. Guinness Son & Co. Ltd.	Guinness Malaysia Berhao	Tuborgs Bryggerier A/S	
Tsingtao	Dublin	Petaling Jaya	Hellerup-Kopenh	
VR China	Ireland	Malaysia	Denmark	
24.00	28.00	29.00	30.00	
18.00	11.80	17.20	18.80	g/100 g
5.55	3.89	5.64	5.59	g/100 g
7.59	4.25	6.61	8.33	g/100 g
868.60	918.60	877.50	860.80	g/1,000 g
683.00	434.00	650.00	715.00	kcal/1,000 g
2,856.00	1,818.00	2,718.00	2,991.00	kJ/1,000 g
7.60	4.20	7.00	6.00	g/L
259.00	61.00	143.00	51.00	mg/L
539.00	300.00	675.00	547.00	mg/L
624.00	597.00	770.00	676.00	mg/L
43.00	18.00	23.00	47.00	mg/L
35.00	32.00	14.00	47.00	mg/L
181.00	86.00	161.00	117.00	mg/L
476.00	273.00	368.00	317.00	mg/L
120.00	132.00	85.00	158.00	mg/L
222.00	208.00	268.00	258.00	mg/L
n.b.	n.b.	n.b.	n.b.	mg/L
28.00	17.00	8.00	12.00	mg/L
0.21	0.23	0.09	0.05	mg/L
1.08	0.23	0.23	0.36	mg/L
0.45	0.22	0.35	0.14	mg/L
0.30	0.07	0.10	0.01	mg/L
74.00	26.00	66.00	184.00	µg/L
460.00	453.00	847.00	383.00	µg/L
385.00	469.00	530.00	987.00	µg/L
2,013.00	1,347.00	1,733.00	1,720.00	µg/L
8,330.00	6,867.00	9,500.00	10,460.00	µg/L
15.00	13.00	8.00	23.00	µg/L
86.00	105.00	139.00	46.00	mg/L
210.00	92.00	256.00	240.00	mg/L
118.00	84.00	82.00	97.00	mg/L
65.00	202.00	286.00	70.00	mg/L
34.00	63.00	306.00	61.00	mg/L
29.00	227.00	159.00	160.00	mg/L
14.00	25.00	48.00	47.00	mg/L
448.00	320.00	628.00	329.00	mg/L
123.00	182.00	104.00	194.00	mg/L
25.00	40.50	60.00	31.00	BE
n.b.	0.56	0.49	0.46	g/100 g
2,074.00	1,267.00	1,605.00	1,719.00	mg/L
10.10	28.60	42.00	15.20	mg/L
11.40	17.40	25.90	16.00	mg/L
70.60	63.10	106.10	84.20	mg/L
16.30	32.70	66.60	53.00	mg/L
33.70	16.00	27.70	31.60	mg/L
2.00	0.70	2.50	1.80	mg/L
11.00	10.30	3.30	4.80	mg/L
0.07	0.11	0.13	0.05	mg/L
0.01	0.01	0.04	0.02	mg/L
1.00	2.00	7.00	8.00	mg/L
4.35	3.99	3.97	4.56	pH
1.95	1.72	2.23	2.38	cP
73.00	80.20	77.40	70.40	Vs. GV %
79.80	80.30	77.40	70.40	EVs. GV %
242.00	164.00	237.00	310.00	EBC

The present-day resurgence of the local brewery in the United States, this time in the form of brewpubs and microbreweries, has revitalized the interest in stouts. From its early beginnings at the Irish breweries of Dublin and Cork, to the English versions, to the current styles of the microbrewing scene, stout has remained a cornerstone of brewing. In celebration of this wonderful history, almost every brewpub or taproom that I visit now in the United States has at least one tap dedicated to some version of stout (appendix). Whether these are truly stouts by some traditional definition is not important, but what is important is the new interest in the wonderful world of stout. As a brewer I am ecstatic that no brewpub or taproom now seems complete without at least one tap flowing the dark and creamy stuff.

The latest technology in stouts is the special device made to dispense the beer from a can with a distinctive and traditional pub foam head. This technology is fully described in chapter 5. But who would have thought that even our own Miller Brewing Company would produce and market an excellent stout, made with all malt and roasted grains and an ale yeast, under their Reserve label — Reserve Velvet Stout?

3

Commercial Brewing of Stouts

BREWING WATER

Although the only real requirement of brewing water, quantitatively the primary component of all beers, is that it be potable (meets drinking standards), Dublin stouts, Burton pale ales, and Pilsen lagers represent different beers brewed classically with quite different waters. I have often wondered, if we began brewing today, whether regional and specialty beers based on local practices and raw materials such as water would arise in today's society. I'm frankly a bit skeptical. Our culture is so full of homogenizing influences of all sorts, and consumers' tastes and preferences are so much influenced by advertising power, that locale as a factor doesn't have much of a chance. To play Devil's advocate, with enough advertising promotion we might agree that Pilsen porters or London pale ales are best. I generally recommend that craft brewers first use the local water *as is* for making their beers rather than trying to change it to some traditional formulation. My thought is that a wonderful new product might arise in this way. Water is certainly local, perhaps the only local ingredient, and

TABLE 3.1

London Water
$(Ca^{++} + Mg^{++}) : CO_3^{--} = 100 : 86$

	IONS		SALTS			
	Millivals	Parts per 100,000		N/1,000	Parts per 100,000	Grains per gallon
Sodium, Na^{++}	1.05	2.4	NaNO$_3$	0.05	0.4	0.3
Magnesium, Mg^{++}	0.30	0.4	NaCl	0.50	2.9	2.0
Calcium, Ca^{++}	4.50	9.0	Na$_2$SO$_4$	0.50	3.6	2.5
Nitrate, NO$_3^-$	0.05	0.3	MgSO$_4$	0.30	1.8	1.3
Chloride, Cl$^-$	0.50	1.8	CaSO$_4$	0.40	2.7	1.9
Sulphate, SO$_4^{--}$	1.20	5.8	CaCO$_3$	4.10	20.5	14.4
Carbonate, CO$_3^{--}$	4.10	12.3	—	—	—	—
	—	32.0	—	—	31.9	22.4

Dublin Water
$(Ca^{++} + Mg^{++}) : CO_3^{--} = 100 : 97$

	IONS		SALTS			
	Millivals	Parts per 100,000		N/1,000	Parts per 100,000	Grains per gallon
Sodium, Na$^+$	0.05	0.1	NaNO$_3$	0.05	0.4	0.3
Magnesium, Mg^{++}	1.60	1.9	MgCl$_2$	0.05	0.2	0.1
Calcium, Ca^{++}	4.00	8.0	MgSO$_4$	0.10	0.6	0.4
Nitrate, NO$_3^-$	0.05	0.3	MgCO$_3$	1.45	6.1	4.3
Chloride, Cl$^-$	0.05	0.1	CaSO$_3$	4.00	20.0	14.0
Sulphate, SO$_4^{--}$	0.10	0.5	—	—	—	—
Carbonate, CO$_3^{--}$	5.45	16.4	—	—	—	—
	—	27.3	—	—	27.3	19.1

Source: Information taken from H. S. Corran, "Source Materials for the History of Brewing," *The Brewer* (October 1974): 583–41.

using it without change is the easiest and least costly brewing strategy. If beer faults accrue that are attributable to water they will be minor ones, water composition can be fixed easily at some later stage.

It might therefore be worthwhile to spend a little time on water chemistry and explore why some waters are preferred for stout brewing. However, it is important to note that of the stout brewers who responded to our survey (chapter 5), few admitted to making any adjustments to the water they specifically used for brewing stout. This includes the Guinness brewers at Park Royal who use Thames Valley Water Authority water as delivered, quoting its similarity to Dublin water (table 3.1).[11] They do adjust the water for lager brewing, however. A few brewers noted that their water is treated with lime. Although this implies alkalizing the water, such treatment is usually used to soften water and remove bicarbonates as follows:

$$Ca(OH)_2 + Ca(HCO_3)_2 = 2CaCO_3 \text{ (precipitates)} + 2H_2O$$

This supports my general view that brewers have plenty to worry about before the water!

The pH of brewing water is not important in itself because water pH is established only by the dissociation of the bicarbonate ion. There are other salts in water that do not affect water pH but react in the mash, affecting *mash* pH. Therefore, the pH of the water is much less important than its content of dissolved salts because the *combined* action of these salts determine how the water will react in the mash. In effect, it is possible to have two waters with an equally alkaline pH, such as pH 8.5, one of which might be strongly alkalizing in the mash and the other weakly alkalizing. Obviously, the first water is high in sodium and bicarbonate ions because these affect water pH. The second water, an ale water for example, would have the alkaline ions balanced with calcium ions in the form of salts of strong acids such as $CaSO_4$ or $CaCl_2$. These neutral salts do not affect water pH but have an acidifying reaction *in the mash* which balances the alkalinity of the bicarbonate. Brewing water is the only significant source of calcium ions in brewing.

The alkaline reaction of bicarbonate is familiar to us in its use as an antacid (e.g., Alka-Selzer) and is easily expressed chemically as:

$$NaHCO_3 + HCl = NaCl + CO_2 \text{ (burp)} + H_2O$$
$$\text{or } HCO_3^- + H^+ = CO_2 + H_2O$$
$$\text{or } CO_3^{--} + 2H^+ = CO_2 + H_2O$$

In either expression the acid, represented by HCl (hydrochloric acid) or H^+, is eliminated. One equivalent of bicarbonate ion eliminates one equivalent of acid.

The acidifying action of Ca^{++} is less straightforward and more dramatic because it involves upsetting one of the buffering systems in wort by effectively changing its concentration. Ca^{++} reacts primarily with the phosphate in malt, which contains plenty of phosphate. In the solution in the mash, the malt's phosphate will adopt all the following ionic forms with some occurring, depending on the pH, in high concentration:

$$H_3PO_4 \rightleftharpoons H_2PO_4^- \rightleftharpoons HPO_4^{--} \rightleftharpoons PO_4^{---}$$

At wort pH HPO_4^{--} is present in highest concentration. Therefore, a simpler expression for the dissociation of the ionic species is:

$HPO_4^{--} \rightleftharpoons PO_4^{---} + H^+$

Ca^{++} forms an insoluble salt with PO_4^{---}. If Ca^{++} is added to the mash in the water or to the kettle in the form of Burton salts (gypsum), insoluble $Ca_3(PO_4)_2$ forms to disturb the equilibrium to the right which releases H^+ (acid) as follows:

$$2HPO_4^{--} + 3Ca^{++} = Ca_3(PO_4)_2 \text{ (precipitates)} + 2H^+$$

If $CaSO_4$ or $CaCl_2$, both neutral salts, are present in brewing water the following reaction might be written for the mash:

$$2K_2HPO_4 + 3CaSO_4 = Ca_3(PO_4)_2 + 2K_2SO_4 + H_2SO_4 \text{ (sulphuric acid)}$$
alkaline   neutral   insoluble   neutral   acid

What of $3Ca_2CO_3$? Will it have an alkalizing or acid-ifying reaction?

$3Ca^{++}$ reacts with $2HPO_4$ to give $Ca_3(PO_4)_2 + 2H^+$
$3CO_3^{--}$ reacts with (and removes) $6H^+$ to give $3CO_2$ and $3H_2O$

Similarly $3HCO_3^-$ removes $3H^+$ to give $3CO_2$ and $3H_2O$. Thus one chemical equivalent of calcium and one equivalent of bicarbonate are not equal to each other in their pH-affecting reactions. Kolbach[13] makes the point that the calcium concentration (expressed in millivals) should be divided by 3.5 when calculating the residual or effective alkalinity of water. Thus a water might contain quite a bit of Ca^{++} as gypsum and be alkalizing in the mash if bicarbonate is present. Indeed all brewing waters, even Burton-on-Trent water, are at least slightly alkalizing in the mash.

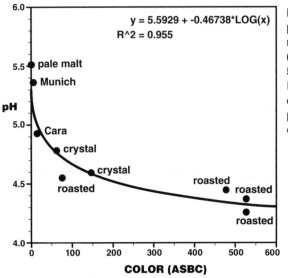

Figure 3.1.
pH of CWE of malts vs. color (5g fine grind/ 50 mL water). Relation of malt color/roasting and pH of a cold water extract of the malt.

Residual alkalinity = total alkalinity – calcium ion/3.5 – magnesium ion/7.0 when all ions are expressed as millivals (total alkalinity = bicarbonate ion)

Why the concern over alkalinity when brewing stout? The colored malts and especially the roasted material are much more acidic than the same amount, by weight, of pale malt (see figure 3.1). The water therefore has an important neutralizing effect on the roasted material. When stouts were brewed with gypsum (Ca_2SO_4 "ale"), Pilsen, or Dublin types of water in our pilot brewery, the mash pH was 4.9, 5.1, and 5.3 respectively. Water that contained a high level of alkaline salts extracted more color and flavor from roasted materials and bitterness from hops, and yielded stouts with a higher pH than when gypseous (ale) water or distilled water (see table 1, chapter 5) was used. This well-known effect was confirmed by the survey of stout brewers.

STOUT BREWING

The survey of stout brewers in chapter 5 revealed that, except for the inclusion of roasted materials, most stouts are made by rather conventional ale brewing methods. These techniques are doubtless familiar to most readers of this book and hardly need further explanation or exploration. Ordinary infusion mash tuns or temperature program systems using stirred vessels and lauter tubs are common.

There is, of course, one stout brewing enterprise of unique interest because of the seminal position the product holds in the world of stouts and in the world beer market. Though the following description and the survey data that follows in chapter 5 probably cover the range of stout brewing practices worldwide, the account given here is largely based on the Guinness process.[10] The reason for this choice is that Guinness is the quintessential stout available everywhere and most readers will have tasted the Guinness Stout. The processes used by this company are typical of contemporary brewing methods used in ale and lager breweries worldwide, but these methods have developed quite recently from unusual, if not extraordinary, traditional practices, so that a discussion of this product alone covers a wide range of stout brewing methods. For example, at the St. James's Gate and London Park Royal breweries Guinness formerly operated traditional (though very large) mash tuns, called kieves, in the brew house. By 1979 in Dublin, these vessels were replaced by mash mixers using a temperature program mash and valley bottom lauter tubs. At Park Royal twin mash conversion vessels (mash mixers) now serve one Meura 2001 mash filter (the latest technology for mash separation). The kieves are still at the brewery though they are no longer in use. It might be

45

useful to recall the old way of brewing and compare it to contemporary methods. This comparison will cover the span between traditional and contemporary technology and the range of technology likely to be used in stout brewing worldwide.

RAW MATERIALS

Stouts are made from malts, roasted materials, and adjuncts. The malt in British stout brewing is typical traditional pale ale malt kilned off (cured) at 176 to 221 degrees F (80 to 105 degrees C) and as low as 1 to 2 percent moisture. The diastatic power (DP) is quite low — about 60 to 80 °L (table 3.2)[12] — but this pale malt, comprising some 60 to 70 percent of the grist, is the only source of amylase in the stout mash. In the case of infusion mashing (in the kieves), this put considerable pressure on the brewer to establish an appropriate and even temperature throughout the mash by judicious mashing of the cool malt with the hot mash water. Uneven mashing-in resulted in hotter and cooler spots in the mash. Of course, in hot spots the low DP malt is likely to lose its enzyme activity which might result in lower extract and/or leave starchy worts. These problems are considerably ameliorated today in mashes that start at a low temperature.

Roasted barley (and/or roasted malt) is the mash component that makes stouts different from pale ales. The Maillard reaction — named for a French chemist — is responsible for the unique colors and flavors that characterize stout products. The Maillard reaction takes place between amines (amino acids and proteins) and carbonyls (sugars and starch), under the influence of heat and moisture. Certainly roasted malt and roasted barley differ in flavor because of the different substances they contain which take part in the Maillard reaction.

TABLE 3.2

Traditional English Pale Malts

	Spratt-Archer*	Plumage-Archer*
Moisture %	1.500	1.800
Extract, lb. 336 lb.	100.500	100.600
Color, 1-inch cell	4.500	4.000
Cold water extract %	18.000	18.700
Diastatic Activity, L°	36.000	37.000
$[a]_D$ of wort solids	118.500	119.000
Extract, on dry malt	102.000	102.400
Total N % on dry malt	1.342	1.314
P.S.N. % on dry malt	0.510	0.509
P.S.N. % on total N	38.000	38.700
P.S.N. % on wort solids	0.670	0.670
1,000-corn dry weight, grams	35.300	38.000
Calculated extract	102.100	102.400
Extract index	108.600	108.000

*These varieties are no longer in use.

Note: (1) Extract values are expressed as "brewers pounds per quarter" which recalculate to roughly 80 percent yield in today's parlance. (2) $[a]_D$ is the specific rotation of polarized light by the wort; maltose has an unusually high and positive $[a]_D$ compared to other wort sugars. (3) Color is by Lovibond Tintometer. (4) Extract index is calculated from the data in the table using Bishop's equation for prediction of malt extract yield and gives the value "A" in that formula. This actual value can be used for comparison to the expectation for "A" of these barley varieties.

Source: Information taken from H. Lloyd Hind, *Brewing Science and Practice*, vol. 1 (London: Chapman Hall, 1950): 254.

Only roasted malt is used by Guinness for export beer. But for other beers, Guinness uses either roasted malt or roasted barley, and they have not been able to detect a flavor difference between these two roasted products (Robert Letters, personal communication).

At the Guinness Park Royal Brewery in London, barley is roasted in a device similar to a coffee roaster (figure

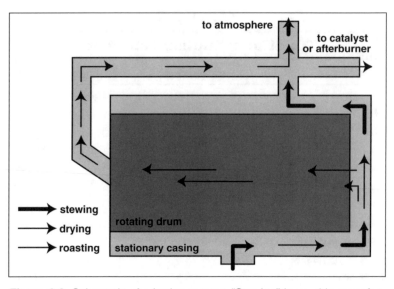

Figure 3.2. Schematic of a barley roaster. "Stewing" is used in manufacture of crystal malts, not roasted barley in which case air passes through the rotating drum as well as around it.

3.2), which takes the material to about 428 degrees F (220 degrees C) in one hundred minutes (figure 3.3) by using hot air from burners. At the appropriate moment, judged by the experienced operator, the barley is quenched and cooled with a charge of water. After further cooling with air, the material is then sent to storage. Roasted barley comprises around 9 percent of the grist for making Guinness, and this is probably quite typical of British stouts. At the St. James's Gate brewery roasted barley is extracted separately from the mash and the extract is added to the pale wort at the kettle. However, at Park Royal finely milled roasted material is included in the mash. Some American craft-brewed stouts undoubtedly contain more than 9 percent of this component and many also contain roasted malt.

Flaked barley could make up to 30 percent of the total cereals used in the grist because the pale malt has sufficient amylolytic capacity to convert this much additional adjunct starch. The barley also could contribute some ß-amylase to the mash. In practical operation, including about 15 percent flaked barley is more typical.

Barley is considerably cheaper than malt. Though it contains little flavor and is weak in amino acids it could contribute its own qualities to stout character based on the high concentration of ß-glucans present. ß-glucans are high molecular weight polymers of glucose linked together by ß1-3 and ß1-4 bonds. The glucans have a positive effect on foam stability, and they easily enhance mouthfeel or beer texture. Too much ß-glucan, however, can cause hazes, jelly-like precipitates, and excessive viscosity, making filtration difficult. This can be controlled with the addition of ß-glucanases or by substituting centrifuges for filtration.

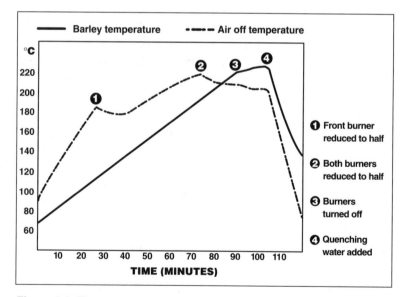

Figure 3.3. Time temperature details typical of producing roasted barley.

Flaked barley is made by steaming barley until it contains about 22 percent moisture and then by passing it between heated steel rollers. It is then dried. The flaked barley is not further milled in the Dublin brewery because it is already crushed in manufacture.

Oatmeal stouts may contain rolled oats in small amounts (about 5 percent of the grist) but the flavor effect of this is likely to be small because of the overriding presence of the roasted material. When we made an experimental beer with pale malt and 30 percent oats, the beer had an unfilterable haze, grainy flavor, and an intensely astringent mouthfeel; it was not a particularly pleasant beer. There was not a unique *flavor* effect from the oats. Adding the oats primarily affected mouthfeel (e.g., astringency). Milk stouts might contain some small percentage of lactose (milk sugar) but not necessarily.

Stout brewers use the full range of hop products available to the modern brewer, including whole ("leaf" or "cone") hops, hop pellets, kettle extracts, and isomerized hop extract for post-fermentation bittering. These are not necessarily used in any unique fashion by stout brewers except that stouts usually contain high bitterness levels, generally forty to seventy IBUs. Such bitter impact would of course fit somewhere between robust and intolerable in a pale beer, but in stouts, with the effective flavor balance of the roasted material, these levels of bitterness are necessary for balance and are pleasant. A typical modern high alpha hop in current use in Britain is Target. The traditional Guinness brewing process used whole hops in an unusual way in the brew house, but today hop pellets and extracts are used and, in Dublin, isomerized hop extract is used to adjust final beer bitterness. The use of several sources of bitterness is common in modern brewing and stout brewers are no exception. Only a few brewers in our survey used late hopping for aroma. Late hop character is not a usual feature of stouts.

PROCESSES OF STOUT BREWING

Milling. The mash tuns (called kieves at Guinness) in use until 1979 required malt that was relatively coarsely milled to assure adequate run-off rates and sufficient extract recovery from these very broad (thirty feet) and deep (grain bed of five feet) vessels. Relatively simple four-roll Porteus mills sufficed for processing malt, and similar mills were devoted to crushing roasted barley to a finer particle size for adequate color extraction. The very well-modified, friable, and very dry malt — when milled coarsely — leaves the husk quite intact and the endosperm as coarse grits with a minimum of flour. This process promotes easier extract recovery and wort run-off from a mash tun; milling the malt too finely reduced the rate of wort recovery.

Today at the Park Royal Brewery the modern Meura 2001 mash filter demands an entirely different approach to milling. Because the bed depth in the mash filter is only four inches or so and the bed can be squeezed with a bladder expanded by air pressure, fine particles are preferred for rapid and complete recovery of extract and efficient sparging. A hammer mill (figure 3.4) has therefore replaced the traditional roll mill. In a hammer mill rapidly revolving and pivoting hammers powder the grist against the wall of the mill. Then milled materials exit the mill through a screen or sieve which controls the size of the particles produced. The malt, roasted barley, and flaked barley are all hammer milled for processing with the pressure mash filter. This mash filter is said to be capable of yielding theoretical amounts of extract

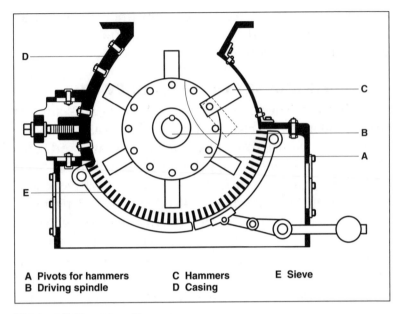

| A Pivots for hammers | C Hammers | E Sieve |
| B Driving spindle | D Casing | |

Figure 3.4. Hammer mill.

and bright wort with normal flavor character. This might be a surprising result given the usual advice to brewers that excessively milled husk contributes too much polyphenol and astringency to wort and causes a high ß-glucan content. Nevertheless, this kind of mash filter appears to work very effectively and is an important advance in brewing technology.

Mashing. Some fascinating practices developed around the traditional kieves. The water and cereal ("liquor and grist") were brought together in a Steele's Masher which gently mixed these two components evenly to form a thick but thoroughly wetted mash. At the Dublin brewery the mash entered the cast iron kieves (there were twenty-four of them) with an unusually low liquid-to-solid ratio of 2.1 to 1 (or rather more than four pounds per gallon). This situation might be expected to favor enzyme survival but also encourage less than fully fermentable worts and low extract recovery. Such a mash was buoyant because of the dense first worts produced. This undoubtedly helped the operation in the deep kieves, especially wort run-off. The mash-in temperature was 148 degrees F (64.5 degrees C). Mashing started at midnight and each brew took some eighteen hours to complete. After a stand of seventy minutes, the taps below the false bottom of the kieves were opened and wort run-off started. Sparging followed immediately using water at 176 degrees F (80 degrees C) to raise the temperature of the mash somewhat during sparging and thus recover the extract more completely and easily. Of course the first worts were much stronger than those that followed and were run off relatively slowly. Medium-strength worts and finally the weak worts emerged from the kieves much later. If one brew filled one kettle as in most modern breweries, including stout breweries, a Guinness brewer would have to wait an inordinate length of time to start the boil. Therefore, the first worts filled the kettles, or coppers (there were ten of them with a normal working capacity of about 800 to 950 hectoliters), and were brought to the boil as soon as they were charged. The later worts from the kieves were diverted to underbacks and upperbacks where the temperature was maintained as the worts waited for an empty kettle for boiling. The stronger and weaker worts were therefore boiled separately in this system, and the final wort gravity was not established until the worts were blended into the fermenters; this is a partigyle system of brewing.

In the Dublin and London breweries today the contrast is quite extreme and similar to contemporary brewing practices in most modern ale and lager breweries. In

London, however, the hammer-milled grain enters twin mash conversion vessels of 500-hectoliter capacity, each capable of producing nearly 1,100 hectoliters of wort per brew into the kettles through the pressure mash filter. The temperature program begins at about 144 degrees F (62 degrees C) with added ß-glucanase to moderate the ß-glucans of the finely milled barley. The temperature is then raised slowly to the same temperature as was used in the kieves, 148 degrees F (64.5 degrees C) for starch conversion. The mashing and wort separation system permits about ten to twelve brews per day with approximately a two-hour cycle time. The efficiency of this system in terms of extract yield is superior to the kieves. At the Park Royal Brewery it is amazing to observe the huge area devoted to the kieves (which are still in place and, incidentally, built originally as a copy of the Dublin brewery) in contrast to the compact apparatus of the modern age. One can but admire and even regret the passing of the robust and straightforward technology of the last century. Fortunately, the modern microbrewing industry of the United States is preserving that technology on a small scale.

Boiling. There was insufficient kettle capacity to boil all the wort produced from the kieves at one time. This led to the partigyle system of brewing where strong worts with a specific gravity of 1.100 or so were boiled first. Weaker worts, usually having SG 1.020, were boiled later with, interestingly enough, the hops recovered from the first boil. The boiling time was one and a half hours. The charge of fresh whole hops was added to the strong worts when the copper kettle was about two-thirds full — some time before the intense "full rolling boil." The addition of the hops to the worts before boiling point probably helped to control kettle foaming as well as hop extraction. The vigorous boil concentrated the wort about 5 percent, sterilized it, precipitated unwanted proteins and extracted and isomerized the alpha-acids of the hops. The final pH of the product was then established by the reactions of water components. After boiling, the wort was "cast" into the hop back where it settled. The wort was then drawn off through the hop bed which served to filter out the hot break. Hops are less well extracted and isomerized in strong worts than in weak ones, and so hops (and the attendant hot break) recovered from the hop back were used again at least once by boiling with the weaker worts. As there was no protection of these recovered hops from air, some oxidation of hop components could have taken place before they were reused. Thus, in the second boil with weak wort, not only was the extraction likely to be more efficient but also different components might have been available for extraction. The partigyle system might therefore lay some claim to being the cause of some unique qualities in beers using that system. However, it is unlikely that this is the case with Guinness or other modern brewers because the technique was abandoned in the late 1970s when wort collection was matched with kettle and whirlpool capacity.

Wort cooling. Originally hot hopped wort from the hop backs was pumped to the roof of the brewery where shallow rectangular one-thousand-hectoliter, open cooling vessels were located. Here the wort began to cool and additional particles, including some cold break (which forms at quite high a temperature), had the opportunity to settle out. The wort then flowed by gravity through counter-current plate heat exchangers, in which the temperature was reduced to 64.5 degrees F (18 degrees C) for fermentation, and then to the storehouse where the fermenters were located. The heat exchangers yielded hot water recovered for brewing. The cooled wort was aerated with sterile air and yeast was added. Conventional heat exchangers are contemporary technology at Guinness and in most modern ale and stout breweries.

Fermentation. Stout fermenters used around the world are of many sizes and designs, ranging from traditional, small, open fermenting squares to large cylindro-conical vessels. Obviously large vessels are only useful to those stout brewers with substantial volume. Original Guinness fermenters were either square or rectangular. The largest of these was rectangular and accommodated twelve thousand hectoliters (2 1/4 million British pints) in a single fermentation. The brewery guides enjoyed reminding visitors that 26 2/3 double decker buses could be accommodated in this vessel (Robert Letters, personal communication). When all the worts of different gravities were transferred to the fermenter they were mixed by rousing with air from the bottom of the fermenter before "dipping" for excise (tax) determination and to assure even wort composition. Before fermentation started, a small volume (about three hundred hectoliters per day) of wort containing yeast was set aside and chilled to 39 to 43 degrees F (4 to 6 degrees C) to prevent fermentation. This was the "gyle" which was added to stout after the primary fermentation was complete to condition it — that is, mature its flavor and add carbonation. The gravity of worts in the fermenter was either an original gravity (OG) of 1.032, 1.045 or 1.073 ("high gravity"). This strategy permitted flexible blending of products toward the end of the process. This has been simplified recently; as in most breweries around the world, high-gravity brewing is now used in which wort at 15 to 17 °Plato is fermented and later diluted with water to trade gravity as required.

Although the square fermenters have been replaced with modern cylindroconical vessels in Dublin and London, the conditions of fermentation have not changed much from the traditional process. The initial wort temperature of about 63 degrees F (17 to 18 degrees C) encouraged rapid onset of fermentation with a temperature rise to at least 74 degrees F (23 degrees C) and occasionally as high as 80 degrees F (27 degrees C). This rapid fermentation typical of ale brewing was complete in some thirty-six to forty-eight hours. These times and temperatures are probably quite typical of contemporary stout brewers everywhere and are only slightly moderated by considerations of vessel geometry or yeast strain.

Most stout brewers, including Miller Brewing Company with their new Reserve Velvet Stout, use a pure strain of *Saccharomyces cerevisiae*, the classical ale yeast. In small vessels this yeast rises to the surface and can be recovered for reuse by "skimming." Traditionally ale brewers probably maintained the constancy of their mixed cultures by skimming because rising to the surface is a somewhat unusual capability for microorganisms. By continually recovering yeast that cropped to the top at a certain defined time during the fermentation, ale and stout brewers therefore conserved their yeast as a stabilized mixed culture. Several of the stout brewers who responded to our survey use their regular lager yeast for making stout. In cylindroconical fermenters ale strains usually separate at the bottom of the vessel and can be recovered from the cone. Most stout brewers, like other ale brewers, use one of these common strategies for yeast use and recovery. However, Guinness at the Park Royal Brewery has selected from its original mixed strain of yeasts a pure ale yeast that is non-flocculent — meaning it neither settles nor rises to the surface in their large 2,000- or 3,500-hectoliter cylindroconical fermenters.

Though Dublin has always used a flocculent head-forming ale yeast, at both breweries the beer is centrifuged to recover yeast for pitching. The Park Royal Brewery, in common with most brewers, introduces a new yeast culture every two to three months. This practice is probably typical of stout brewers, except for more traditional operations where the yeast is replaced considerably less often or only as needed as indicated by yeast performance or deterioration of flavor. In those breweries that use the same yeast for many different products, the yeast used for stout fermentations is probably the oldest yeast in the brewery and is discarded after use in a stout fermentation.

Finishing practices (tunnage). At this stage former processes at Guinness and their current practices are very similar. When fermentation was complete after some thirty-six to forty-eight hours, depending on temperature and wort gravity, the stout was moved (or "tunned") from the storehouse to the vathouse (called "tunnage" at Guinness). Upon leaving the fermenters, the stout passed through a centrifuge to remove the vast bulk of the yeast and any other particulate matter. Then the beer was chilled to about 47 degrees F (8 to 9 degrees C) before (Park Royal) or after (Dublin) centrifugation.

In order to achieve the necessary throughput capacity several centrifuges operated in parallel. Because the yeast multiplied up to five times its original amount during fermentation, there was considerable excess yeast remaining after sufficient yeast was set aside for future needs. Although centrifuges are efficient for removing yeast and protein particles from beers, they are not perfect, and some particles remain to be removed by another mechanism.

Therefore, as the stout exited the centrifuge a small amount (about 1.5 ppm) of cold isinglass finings — primarily a collagen from the dried swim bladders of some fish (particularly sturgeon) dissolved in a weak acid — was added. Finings have a positive charge and help flocculate the negatively charged yeast cells and protein particles into larger clumps that settle more rapidly. The stout was then held at a temperature of about 44 degrees F (7 degrees C) in the vats of the vathouse for a minimum of five days. During this time the stout began to mature in flavor, with the diacetyl (buttery or butterscotch) and acetaldehyde (green or bruised apple) flavor characters beginning to fade. In the vathouse the brews of each day were kept separate. The brews were called on for blending and make-up into the racking vats.

Today, the use of short-term cold storage in the presence of some yeast for flavor maturation and the use of finings for clarification are quite common among ale breweries (including stout brewers), especially in Britain where isinglass finings have a long and useful history. However, in more traditional breweries centrifuges are unusual. They operate best when there is a large and rather continuous throughput of beer. Centrifuges are compact and avoid exposing the beer to filtration — a process that might remove color or flavor materials, for example, as well as being somewhat inefficient because of the beer viscosity ascribed to the ß-glucans present in stouts. Centrifuges can also damage some yeasts, warm up the product, produce a lot of noise, and can require a good deal of electrical energy. Stout brewers, therefore, typically use flocculent yeast for removal of yeast during and after fermentation. This is followed by cold storage, often with the addition of finings, for clarification by settlement and flavor maturation. Typically these processes are followed by filtration to clarify the products. Maturation and conditioning periods for all stouts are generally short (days not weeks). For most ale and stout brewers today, including Guinness, only dilution from fermentation gravity to that required for trade, carbonation, and packaging would now remain to complete the process.

Blending and conditioning. Most commercial beers are blended for packaging, which aids in consistency and has other advantages. However, each of the individual brews contributing to such a blend is treated in nominally the same way at most breweries, including the Guinness breweries today. In contrast, former practice at Dublin took selected stouts available in the vathouse, fermented at different original wort gravities (1.032, 1.045, and 1.073), and blended them into the racking vats depending on the stout in demand for packaging. This permitted several advantages, including flexibility and consistency at blending (called "make-up"). For example, as required by the market, draught stout, at a final OG of 1.044, and porter, at OG 1.035, could be produced. At this make-up stage, the gyle (fresh cold wort containing yeast) was blended into the stout at perhaps 5 percent of the total volume and was responsible for carbonation during refermentation in the cask or bottle. In the Draught Guinness process, introduced in the 1960s, this secondary fermentation was, and continues to be, carried out in the brewery.

The final and unique character of Guinness was (and still is) derived in some part from special beers added at make-up. While some added beer is simply reprocessed beer from various in-brewery sources, as is common in most breweries, a small amount of special beer, possibly containing diluted isomerized hop extract, is used to adjust flavors, including the bitterness level.

This special material is used to manufacture Guinness Flavor Essence (GFE) as well. GFE is produced only at the St. James's Gate (Dublin) brewery and is distributed worldwide to franchise brewers to impart the color and unique flavors characteristic of Guinness.

After make-up, the cold stout was moved to the conditioning tanks. During this transfer it was warmed to about 68 degrees F (20 degrees C), causing the yeast and sugar in the gyle to ferment. This conditioning, or secondary fermentation, which was continuously stirred (roused) to keep the yeast in suspension, lasted around seventy-two hours with only about one million yeast cells per milliliter of stout. This fermentation achieved important ends: it carbonated the beer sufficiently; depleted any dissolved oxygen which might later contribute to flavor instability; and removed the last traces of diacetyl and acetaldehyde which might cause "green" or immature flavors. A more rapid conditioning of twenty to thirty hours could, if necessary, be achieved by adding more yeast (up to ten million cells per milliliter) as the blended stout is moved into the conditioning tanks.

While secondary fermentation analogous to the gyle is a common brewing practice (Budweiser and Coors use kraeusen fermentations), it is likely rare among stout brewers.

Pasteurization. After the conditioning fermentation was complete, centrifuges were again used to remove the accumulated yeast. A top pressure of nitrogen was applied to keep air out in a hermetically sealed system that also served to keep the carbon dioxide in. Although stout was not pasteurized in the traditional process, great improvements in technology — like eliminating oxygen pick-up — make it possible today. This practice reduces live yeast and bacteria to vanishingly low levels. Although bacterial spores are not destroyed by this mild heat treatment, such organisms would not normally be expected in beer. Guinness uses bulk or "flash" pasteurization. The advantage of flash pasteurization is that the beer is heated for only a very short time at a relatively high temperature. The combination of high temperature and short time is less damaging to beer flavor than prolonged heating at a lower temperature. Most brewers, including stout producers, pasteurize their products in the final package using a tunnel pasteurizer; however, this is a bulky apparatus. Most British stouts and ales, including Guinness, receive about forty pasteurization units, forty minutes at 140 degrees F (60 degrees C) or the heat equivalent.

Gassing. In the contemporary process pasteurized stout is cooled to 49 degrees F (10 degrees C) and, if necessary, carbonated by injecting carbon dioxide gas into the beer main as the product is being transferred to the racking tank. The amount of carbon dioxide in draught stout is one volume or two grams per liter (compared to 2.6 volumes in many domestic American beers). Because nitrogen is not very soluble in beer, it is also injected to achieve 3 to 5 percent nitrogen by volume using a special vortexing device called a nitrogenator. In the racking tank the stout is subject to a top pressure of twenty-five pounds per square inch gauge (psig) of a gas mixture (60 percent nitrogen and 40 percent carbon dioxide by volume) to prevent gas loss. This is the stout that is packaged in kegs. The mixed gasses are responsible for the famous Guinness foam head. Bottled Guinness is not nitrogenated, but it is instead refermented in the bottle (bottle conditioned) and available *in Ireland* as Guinness Extra Stout. Elsewhere, however, it is carbonated by bulk secondary fermentation with the appropriate amount of gyle as already described and additional carbon dioxide injected as needed. Draught Guinness in the can will be dealt with separately in chapter 5. Mixed gas dispense for draught beers and (mostly) stouts is an intriguing technology, especially in cans, somewhat disparagingly called "widget beers."

4

A Taste of Stout

STOUT AND BEER STYLES

The concept of beer styles fascinates brewers, especially craft brewers and home brewers, because it reminds them of the long history and diverse geographic origins of beers. Alcoholic beverages in general are intimately woven into the social and economic development of humankind in many parts of the world and have helped to define this development.

Beer styles are a small part of that great historical heritage from which we sprang and which defines who we are today. Beer styles are treasured fragments of history and deserve all the respect and loving conservation accorded to any other such links to our past. However, it's important to remember that beer styles of yesteryear are just that — they are, for the most part, of times past — and to overindulge ourselves in contemplation of the origins of beer styles is perhaps to allow the past to get in the way of the present and the future. I have the experience too often that a modern beer is accused of not being a "true" beer style. It might be useful to remind ourselves that the last person to drink such a "true" product probably died half a century or two ago. So I wonder how the critic can (1) be so sure it's not the same; (2) expect it to be the same; and (3) want it to be the same. Similarly, some will say a beer, called "X" by the brewer who made it, is "more of a 'Y'." What gall!

The concept of beer styles also provides brewers, or more correctly marketers of beers, with a rich lode of assumptions, opinions, stereotypes, and assertions to draw upon. When selling beer, these style-words can be used to send the purchaser useful signals about the contents of the bottle, playing not to consumers' knowledge necessarily, but to their assumptions. In the real world of brewing science, however, the concept of beer styles quickly breaks down to an irrelevancy because beers with certain labels from certain regions and even certain breweries rarely fit the stereotypes the beer stylist dictates.

Beer styles were originally based on local tastes and ideas, brewing customs and practices, local raw materials, brewing equipment, and so on, to say nothing of the personalities involved and the physical environment. These days hops, malt, brewing equipment, and ideas are no longer local possessions, nor are they intended to be. They travel the world in the global market and so blur regional and historical differences among beers and contaminate, even destroy, stylistic purity. Beers travel, too, and alter local tastes. Nonetheless, we needed a definition of stout. What is a stout?

We first discarded all the adjectives for stout — Irish, milk, imperial, oatmeal, extra, oyster, and others — as meaningless in analytical or sensory terms. Later we rejected any useful difference in analytical or sensory terms among porters and stouts and other black beers, though some are sweeter than others. These are all simply black beers whose flavor impact is dominated by roasted materials. One brewery's oatmeal stout and another's imperial and another's extra and another's sweet or dry or milk or porter are simply not on any logical continuum in sensory or analytical terms. The definition continued to elude us.

Michael Jackson[5] makes the point that when a brewer makes a porter *and* a stout the porter is generally less "full-bodied" than the stout. When we surveyed commercial stout brewers we asked them how they distinguished among different styles of stouts and separated stout from porter and other black beers. Not one major stout brewer replied to these questions. Either they had no advice to give us or they assumed — an assumption which turned out to be correct — the questions to be irrelevant. In contrast, American craft brewers wrote persuasive pieces on this topic (chapter 5). To conclude, it was not difficult for us to decide that a stout is simply a black beer *called a stout* by the brewer who made it.

THE TASTE OF STOUTS

For our taste trials we acquired all the stouts — using the definition of a black beer *called a stout* — available through major wholesalers in the western states plus a few others acquired through eastern retail outlets. At the time Miller's Velvet Stout was not available and has been omitted. A few breweries abroad graciously sent us samples of product or provided us with their own sensory analysis. We did our best to follow similar methods, especially the descriptors of flavor, so that we could blend these data with our own.

Our taste panel comprised five members, all of whom are knowledgeable about sensory science and are experienced in beer tasting. The panel was organized and led by Susan Langstaff, formerly a graduate student in our research laboratory and now an independent consultant in the field. For our tasting she invented a new method of sensory analysis called "consensus profiling" which allowed the sensory data of the group (rather than that of five individual judges) to be acquired. This method considerably simplified data acquisition, because the group arrived by discussion at a consensus value for each descriptor for each beer. In such a small panel, consensus profiling prevented the extreme views of one judge from upsetting the panel's overall considered view and opinion.

For preparation and training, in one session the panel tasted all the stouts in a round-table format with the label showing. Each judge was responsible for leading the discussion on four stouts. The purpose of this discussion was twofold: first, the panel developed a lexicon of sensory terms (i.e., a set of words, descriptors or a dictionary) by which the judges all agreed they could describe the stouts; second, the panel agreed on which beers represented high, medium, or low intensity for the sensory terms selected. These stouts were set aside for reference to be used during the blind assessment so that each judge could be reminded what terms meant and how to distinguish them. In addition, this preview served as a panel training because it gave the judges useful insight into the range of sensory impacts to be expected in these stouts. The blind tasting followed several days later.

The tasting form that resulted from this exercise required judgment of (1) foam quality, (2) beer aroma, (3) beer flavor, and (4) beer mouthfeel, using some required and some optional terms. These descriptive terms and the identity of beers that best illustrated each term are shown in table 4.1. During the blind tasting, the judges could retrain themselves on the standard stouts (identified only as being the high/low diacetyl

TABLE 4.1

A Lexicon of Terms for Describing Stouts

FOAM

Color	Mackeson Triple Stout (darkest color)
Stability	Guinness Extra Stout (most stable)
Texture*	Guinness Extra Stout (finest bubbles)

FLAVOR (mouth)

Sweet/lingering sweet	Dragon Stout
Bitter/lingering bitter	Grant's Imperial Stout
Burnt/lingering burnt	Rogue Shakespeare Stout
Acidic/sour*	Old Australia Stout
Roast/coffee*	Anderson Valley Oatmeal Stout

AROMA

Overall intensity	
Fruity/floral*	Extreme example: Sierra Nevada Stout
Estery*	
Burnt/roasted	Anderson Valley Oatmeal Stout
Aldehydic*	Samuel Smith's Imperial Stout
Diacetyl*	Steelhead Stout
Acetic	Sheaf Stout

MOUTHFEEL

Alcoholic	Sierra Nevada Stout
Fullness	Samuel Smith's Imperial Stout
Astringency*	Rogue Shakespeare Stout

(* These terms were optional.)

standard, for example) which were available for comparison throughout the tasting. All the stouts were tasted by each judge with several porters and other black beers thrown in for comparison. Water, Budweiser, and crackers were available to refresh the palate between samples, which were served at 55 degrees F (13 degrees C). Each judge first rated the stout in silence on his/her own tasting form and then a discussion was held to agree on the panel's best rating/response. Tasting in this way was a particularly fatiguing exercise and was done over the course of six hours with ample rests between samples. Tough work, but somebody has to do it!

The objective of this tasting was not so much to rate the stouts in terms of our preference or to give descriptions of stouts akin to those wine writers invent for wines, because such information is irrelevant. Instead, our focus was on learning to what extent stouts were related to each other by flavor character and whether there were any natural groupings among stouts based on such factors as national origin or manufacturing practice.

All these descriptors were rated on a nine-point scale. The important thing to remember is that the scale is not absolute and is adapted to stouts. Thus a rating of three in "burnt" implies a fairly low impact of that flavor for a stout and fairly low impact relative to other stouts in the tasting that might score, for example, a seven. This lexicon and rating scale is not applicable to other beer, such as pale beers. To have left enough room on the "burnt" scale to accommodate a beer like Amstel Light as well as Mackeson would have caused all the stout data to scrunch up toward 9.9 to 10 on the scale. Several of the stouts were identified by the panel by name because of the particular characteristics of the product either in flavor (Rogue is high in diacetyl and astringency) or appearance (Guinness has a most stable white head), and these comments have been noted. The beers we tasted are listed in table 4.2.

The flavor lexicon — e.g., the difference between *roasted* and *burnt* — might deserve some comment. Generally speaking, we regarded the two terms as relating

TABLE 4.2

Identification of the Twenty-Three Black Beers

Code	Name of Beer	Code	Name of Beer
1	Lost Coast Stout	13	Samuel Adams Cream Stout
2	Carbine Stout	14	Young's Oatmeal Stout
3	Old Australia Stout	15	Old #38 Stout
4	Watney's Cream Stout	16	Anchor Porter
5	Mendicino Blackhawk Stout	17	Dragon Stout
6	Guinness Extra Stout	18	Sapporo Black Beer
7	Rogue Shakespeare Stout	19	Samuel Smith's Imperial Stout
8	Stallion Stout	20	Sierra Nevada Stout
9	Sheaf Stout	21	Samuel Smith's Taddy Porter
10	Steelhead Stout	22	Anderson Valley Oatmeal Stout
11	Grant's Imperial Stout	23	Mackeson Triple Stout
12	Samuel Smith's Oatmeal Stout		

to the same flavor impact — that of roasted material — but the burnt character was more acrid and ashen and carbonized than the roasted character, which was more coffee and chocolate tasting. In some beers we thought roasted clearly dominated and gave a high score for it and a low one for burnt. In some beers the burnt character was dominant and we gave low values for roasted. In some stouts the impact was more evenly divided between the two, and so we scored it as such. With no way to confirm our assumption, we tended to think of the burnt character as more typical of roasted barley and the roasted quality as coming from black malt. (Note: Guinness does not distinguish a flavor difference between these products [Robert Letters, personal communication]). *Bitter* and *sweet* are very straightforward flavor impacts, and even untrained judges would feel confident they could pick them out and distinguish between them. But these flavor characters strongly interact and sweet beers often taste less bitter than their analysis implies they should. Similarly, very bitter beers, as stouts usually are, often taste as if they have little sweetness. It takes practice to rate sweetness in the presence of bitterness, especially high bitterness and roasted qualities. We found almost all the stouts had significant sweetness (a few were downright sugary) despite the overall impact of bitter and burnt that a more casual judge might report.

The aroma lexicon was intended to reflect *floral*, *fruity*, and *fragrant* characters connected with aromas from fermentation, hopping, and other raw materials. The *aldehydic* character is that of green apples — probably due to the presence of acetaldehyde — and is quite typical in fermented products. All the stouts contained some of this flavor and a few were especially high in this character. *Acetic* tastes and aromas were similarly present to some extent in most stouts, and a few were characterized by this flavor. Though we expected acetic character to be high in some stouts, in a few cases we could not be sure if this was the result of spoilage or deliberate brewing practice. In some stouts the raw material aromas swamped the fragrant/fermentation aromas. In such cases a high rating in *burnt* aroma shows up.

The *alcoholic* character is not necessarily the result of a high-alcohol product, but is a warming sensation in the nose and palate when the beer is smelled or imbibed. It is a sensation more felt than tasted and we have, therefore, listed it as a mouthfeel term, although this is not necessarily good practice. The mouthfeel terms that should be listed separately from flavor include *fullness* (body) and *astringency*. Mouthfeel qualities are separate and different from flavor though not many understand that idea. Thus, a beer with a powerful flavor impact is commonly assigned a high rating for fullness. Rather, fullness is a feeling of heaviness or thickness on the tongue, a viscosity or resistance to movement in the mouth and a mouthfilling sensation (perhaps like drinking cream). Some beers on the stout scale, though flavorful, were not very "full" by this test as we applied it. Astringency is another term that is a mouthfeel sensation, which is a puckering or drying of the oral cavity by the product (like the aftereffect of drinking young red wine). Astringency is distinct from bitterness in beers, but some practice is required to pick it out. We noted those beers we thought showed astringency in significant amounts.

TASTING RESULTS

The correlations among the descriptive terms are shown in table 4.3. The significance of this table is that it reveals the flavor terms that are *statistically* related to each other in this test. This does not necessarily imply a causal relationship, though such a relationship is possible. Diacetyl was significantly present in only one stout and so this term was removed from the matrix (table 4.3). There were seven positive correlations of high statistical significance. We expected that bitter and burnt flavors would correlate since these are related terms with overlapping sensory impact. Similarly the negative correlation between sweet taste and bitter and astringent was expected because they are antagonistic flavors. The negative correlation of roast flavor and burnt flavor expresses our general experience that one or the other character dominated in most stouts. The correlation of fullness with roast flavor, and fragrance with the mouthfeel term alcoholic might also be rationalized. The correlation of aldehydic with sour hints at related fermentation or spoilage problems. The other statistical correlations, which are noted

TABLE 4.3

Correlation Coefficients (r)
Among the Descriptive Terms (df=20)

Term	1	2	3	4	5	6	7	8	9	10	11	12	13	14
Foam Color	1.00	–	–	–	–	–	–	–	–	–	–	–	–	–
Foam Stability	-0.31	1.00	–	–	–	–	–	–	–	–	–	–	–	–
Fragrant	0.37	-0.23	1.00	–	–	–	–	–	–	–	–	–	–	–
Roast Aroma	0.10	-0.16	0.09	1.00	–	–	–	–	–	–	–	–	–	–
Aldehydic	-0.10	0.35	0.05	-0.49*	1.00	–	–	–	–	–	–	–	–	–
Acetic	0.22	0.42	-0.20	-0.11	0.24	1.00	–	–	–	–	–	–	–	–
Sweet	0.53**	0.06	0.27	-0.22	0.35	0.44**	1.00	–	–	–	–	–	–	–
Sour	-0.01	0.20	0.35	-0.22	0.64**	0.18	0.32	1.00	–	–	–	–	–	–
Bitter	-0.04	-0.24	0.19	0.23	-0.38	-0.27	-0.62**	-0.27	1.00	–	–	–	–	–
Astringent	-0.21	0.09	-0.15	-0.29	0.09	-0.01	-0.42*	0.26	0.39	1.00	–	–	–	–
Burnt Flavor	0.09	0.01	0.19	0.02	-0.28	-0.09	-0.30	-0.06	0.73***	0.40	1.00	–	–	–
Full	0.56**	0.02	0.10	0.28	-0.18	0.31	0.34	-0.21	0.05	-0.36	0.05	1.00	–	–
Alcoholic	-0.03	-0.05	0.47*	0.15	0.04	-0.02	0.16	0.30	0.25	-0.10	0.30	0.32	1.00	–
Roast Flavor	0.12	0.06	-0.01	0.39	-0.09	0.09	0.32	-0.23	-0.41	-0.61**	-0.52	4.49*	0.21	1.00

*, **, ***, r significant at $p < 0.05$, $p < 0.01$ and $p < 0.001$, respectively.

by an asterisk in table 4.3, are more difficult to rationalize and indeed no rational or causal relationship necessarily exists. It appears in this group of beers that burnt, aldehydic, and astringent are undesirable sensory attributes whereas roast aroma and roast flavor are desirable ones.

The statistical method known as Principle Component Analysis (PCA) was used to determine whether or not these stouts could be grouped together in any instructive way by the sensory terms we selected. The PCA also helped us recognize which terms dominate the flavor spectrum and the relationships among those terms. For the twenty-two stouts tasted, the first five Principle Components for the sensory attributes accounted for 80

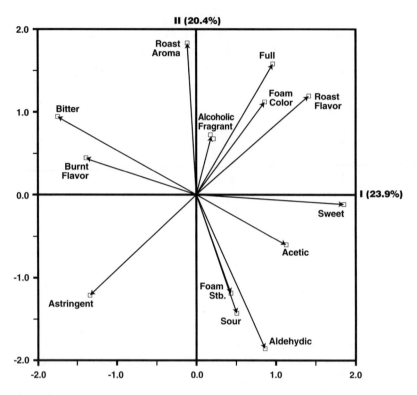

Figure 4.1. Principal Component Analysis of the data for twenty-two stouts for fourteen attributes. The attribute vectors are plotted on the first two Principle Components.

percent of the variability in the data. Specifically, the first and second Principle Components (figure 4.1) accounted for 24 percent and 20 percent, respectively, of the variability. The first and second Principle Components are where we expected to find the sensory qualities that most characterize the samples tested.

In these data the first Principle Component comprised sweet and roast flavor to the right. These qualities were inversely correlated with bitter, astringent, and burnt flavor to the left. Since these vectors in the Principle

Component space are roughly the same length, these terms are all equally useful in describing the differences among these twenty-two stouts. Attributes heavily weighted on the second Principle Component (PC) were roast aroma and full on the one hand and aldehydic on the other. In this data set the first five Principle Components were statistically significant dimensions. Fragrant, alcoholic, and sour were heavily loaded on the third PC, foam stability and acetic on the fourth PC, and foam color on the fifth PC. These terms have all been assembled into figure 4.1. The vectors of figure 4.1 define the sensory qualities of the PC space, therefore the individual beers can be assigned by statistical methods to a location in that space. This process tends to group together stouts with related sensory qualities (see figure 4.2).

Forming a cluster in the section on the left of the Principle Component space — characterized by bitterness, burnt flavor, and astringency — were Grant's Imperial Stout, Watney's Cream Stout, Mendocino Stout, Anchor Porter, Samuel Smith's Imperial Stout, Guinness Extra Stout, and Carbine Stout. Sapporo Black Beer, Old Australia Stout, Samuel Smith's Oatmeal Stout, and Dragon Stout form a cluster in the southeast quadrant and are distinguished by displaying some sweetness, aldehydic character, and acetic aroma or sour flavor. Stallion Stout and Mackeson Triple Stout were best characterized by high sweetness. Samuel Adams Cream Stout, located close to the center of the PC space, might be considered the "average" product. Its neighbors — Old #38, Young's Oatmeal Stout, and Sheaf Stout — displayed somewhat more roast aroma and flavor, fullness, and some sweetness. Samuel Smith's Taddy Porter was a unique product high in astringency, aldehydic, and sour qualities.

Stout

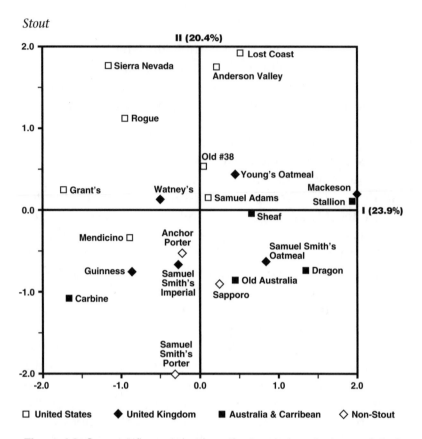

Figure 4.2. Same as figure 1, but here the twenty-two stouts are plotted on the first two Principal Components.

For the most part, those stouts in the northern half and northwest quadrants are American craft-brewed stouts. They do not cluster together in the PC space; rather, the tasting data clearly distinguish them from their imported cousins. They are characterized more by roast, burnt, bitter, and full qualities than are the imports, and they differ from each other more, as a group, than the imports do.

Spiderweb plots are a popular, dramatic, and rather easy way of presenting sensory data and work well when there are only a few samples. Using the spiderweb plot, similarities and differences among the beers are readily apparent. Homebrew clubs and craft brewers who are not now using this method for data presentation might look into using it during tasting events at their meetings.

We present two pieces of data using the spiderweb plot. The first of these, figure 4.3, contains our own data and shows Guinness, Sierra Nevada Stout, and Samuel Smith's Oatmeal Stout. The extreme foam stability of the Guinness, the bitterness/fragrance of the Sierra Nevada Stout, and the sweet/sour character of the Samuel

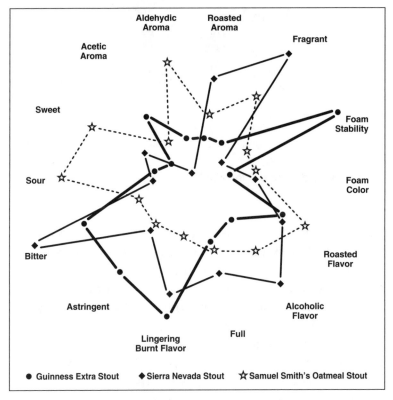

Figure 4.3. Spiderweb plot for Guinness Extra Stout, Samuel Smith's Oatmeal Stout, and Sierra Nevada Stout.

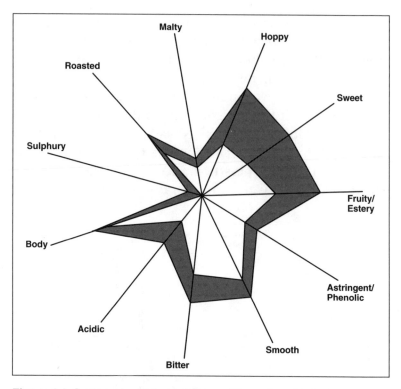

Figure 4.4. Spiderweb plot for variations of three draught stouts.

Smith's Oatmeal Stout jump out of the page dramatically in this data presentation. Yet, figure 4.3 is already too complex to accommodate numerical axes, let alone record the data on all twenty-two stouts we tasted! Indeed, this method of data presentation has its good uses as well as some severe limitations.

The same method was used in figures 4.4 and 4.5. These figures and tables 4.4A and 4.4B were provided by Guinness. The data show sensory and analytical results for three draught and three bottled stouts in the Irish market. Although we do not know which stout is in which keg, stouts A, B, and C in the draught category (see figure 4.4 and table 4.4A) are Guinness, Beamish, and Murphy's. The high-gravity bottled stouts (see figure 4.5 and table 4.4B) are Guinness Foreign Extra Stout, Legend (brewed from maize and sorghum by Nigerian Breweries, Ltd.), and Danish Royal Stout.

In the spiderweb plots the sensory data for all beers fall within the shaded band shown where, for each flavor category, zero (meaning none was detected) is at the center of the web and four (meaning the flavor was strongly detected) is at the periphery. When comparing the two spiderwebs, the draught stouts tend to

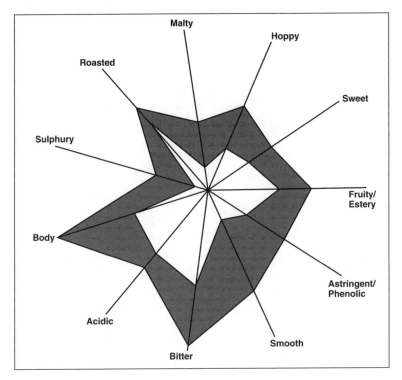

Figure 4.5. Spider web plot for variations of three high gravity stouts.

TABLE 4.4A

A: Draught Stouts

	A	B	C
OG (°P)	9.750	9.090	9.530
Ethanol (% v/v)	4.200	3.880	4.110
EBU	48.000	33.000	37.000
pH	4.000	4.200	3.970
Total Acidity (% w/v) (as acetic acid)	0.097	0.070	0.071
Color (EBC 430nm)	125.000	117.000	124.000
Energy Value (kcal/100 mL)	35.000	33.000	34.000
Fermentation Volatiles (mg/L)			
Ethyl Acetate	12.000	19.000	11.000
Isoamyl Acetate	1.000	3.500	1.400
Propanol	17.000	19.000	11.000
Isobutanol	15.000	33.000	18.000
Isoamyl Alcohols	48.000	71.000	66.000
Acetaldehyde	1.000	1.000	1.000
Diacetyl	0.030	0.080	0.050
2,3-Pentanedione	0.010	0.020	0.020

TABLE 4.4B

B: High Gravity Bottled Stouts

	D	E	F
OG (°P)	17.740	17.670	16.920
Ethanol (% v/v)	7.700	8.000	7.800
EBU	76.000	48.000	37.000
pH	4.050	4.140	3.610
Total Acidity (% w/v) (as acetic acid)	0.195	0.161	0.144
Color (EBC 430nm)	190.000	190.000	207.000
Energy Value (kcal/100 mL)	65.000	65.000	62.000
Fermentation Volatiles (mg/L)			
Ethyl Acetate	29.000	24.000	14.000
Isoamyl Acetate	3.100	2.200	2.300
Propanol	24.000	18.000	19.000
Isobutanol	24.000	21.000	32.000
Isoamyl Alcohols	100.000	116.000	203.000
Acetaldehyde	4.000	3.000	4.000
Diacetyl	0.160	0.180	0.130
2,3-Pentanedione	0.050	0.030	0.010

tilt to the hoppy, sweet, fruity-estery side, whereas in the high-gravity materials the bitter, acidic, body side of the web dominate the flavor profile. They are, therefore, quite different products. The draught stouts (figure 4.4) are similar in many flavor categories — illustrated by the narrow width of the shaded band — with most variations occurring in the hoppy, sweet, and fruity-estery characters. Since these three stouts compete head to head in the same market for the same consumers, some similarities among them might well be anticipated. Judging by the width of the shaded band representing the sensory data, the high gravity stouts differ more among themselves, although it's possible that the curious Nigerian product drives the data. Analytical values for these six products (see tables 4.4A and 4.4B) confirm the sensory data.

In our pilot plant, we brewed nine stouts with three levels of roasted material — 5 percent, 7 percent, and 9 percent at 12 °Plato or OG 1.048 — and three water treatments — $CaSO_4$ (200 milligrams per liter) added to deionized water, deionized water without salts addition, and deionized water compounded to be similar to Dublin water. We previously found these waters increased mash and wort pH, but the effect on beer pH was, as expected, not very great. It is important to remember that the pH scale is logarithmic. Thus, a change of 0.1 pH unit in the wort, which water differences might easily accomplish, and a drop of 1 pH unit from wort to beer pH under the influence of yeast action, represents a hundredfold difference in acidity, or the hydrogen ion concentration. Therefore, we would not expect much contribution to beer pH from brewing water.

We used the "consensus profile" technique for flavor analysis and then looked among the results for significant sensory effects. We found that when additional roasted material was added it increased the roasted and burnt flavor and aroma characters — not a very surprising result! Furthermore, the more alkaline water consistently increased the total sensory bitterness of the stouts, though as far as we could tell it did not much change the sensory quality of that bitterness. These two effects were quite marked, but no other consistent sensory effect of brewing water showed up in these trials. The analytical data for these stouts is printed in table 5.1 in chapter 5.

WHEN YOU TASTE STOUTS

Even the mildest stout, whether commercial or homebrewed, tends to be a big beer. When tasting such beers, controlling the fatigue factor is both important and quite difficult. Fatigue simply means your detectors of aroma and flavor wear out. Such detectors have only so much capacity before their performance (and therefore your performance as a taster) declines. This has two parts: (1) when your sensory receptors simply become fatigued because of the amount of information being received and transmitted; and (2) the familiarity factor where your flavor detection apparatus accustoms itself to the sensory information received and then adjusts its zero setting. This fatigue also shows up in the carry-forward of the sensory impact of one sample to the next. There is not a lot that can be done to minimize these problems, but ignoring them is certainly a most unsatisfactory solution. When tasting you must be in good condition to taste — in good health, in a good mood, with ample time to spend, and an interest in and commitment to the tasting. Don't smoke, not so much for your own tasting ability, but because it disturbs others. Also, the smell of tobacco in clothes as well as other perfumes is a distraction.

TABLE 4.5

A Lexicon of Beer Descriptors

Acetaldehyde	Green apple flavor
Alcohol	Warming, prickly sensation in the mouth and throat
Astringent	Dry, puckery sensation, as in grape skin tannin
Bitter	Sensation generally perceived on the back of the tongue and sometimes roof of the mouth, as with caffeine or hop resin
Body	Not a flavor, but the sensation of viscosity in the mouth, as with thick (full-bodied) beers or thin (light-bodied) beers
Cooked vegetables	See DMS
Diacetyl	Butter or butterscotch-like
DMS (dimethyl sulfide)	Cooked cabbage or sweet corn–like
Fruity-estery	Flavors similar to fruits most commonly found in beers: strawberry, banana, raspberry, apple, pear
Husky-grainy	Raw grainlike flavor; see Astringent
Metallic	Tinny, coinlike, bloodlike
Moldy	A flavor similar to that of moldy bread or unintentionally moldy cheese (refrigerator green mold)
Oxidation	Paper or cardboardlike, winy, sherrylike, rotten pineapple or rotten vegetables
Phenolic	Medicinal, Band-aid, smoky, clovelike, plasticlike
Salty	Sensation generally perceived on the sides of the tongue as with table salt (sodium chloride)
Skunky (light struck)	Like a skunk (the British will refer to this character as "catty" because there are no skunks in the United Kingdom)
Solventlike	Acetone, lacquer thinner
Sour/acidic	Sensation generally perceived on the sides of the tongue, as in lemon juice
Sulfury	Sulfur dioxide, hydrogen sulfide (rotten eggs), yeastlike flavor; see DMS, skunky
Sweet	Sensation generally perceived on the tip of the tongue as with sucrose (white table sugar)

Be sure the place of the tasting is clean, comfortable, organized, quiet, and odor free. Provide palate cleansers such as bread, water, or when tasting dark beers, a very light beer. Select samples that are reasonably well matched and do not sample more than three to five beers in one session. Taste them blind, without the label showing, because the bias introduced by identification overpowers any quantitative measure of flavor quality.

We always taste beer in full-sized, tulip wine glasses for which we have light aluminum covers to entrap the aroma volatiles. Though we have beer glasses of several traditional shapes we reserve these for the full and proper presentation and enjoyment of our products, not serious tasting. We put a reasonable measure of beer in each glass — at least one-third full — for several reasons: to conserve beer temperature, to provide an ample source of volatiles, and to give the taster the opportunity to take beer-sized sips of the products. We provide a standard score card and a pencil (or, these days, training on the computer!) to minimize test anxiety. Within the confine of the tasting room we eschew conversation or exclamations or any other form of communication, verbal and non-verbal. Finally, of course, we taste the sample. To control fatigue, we work quickly with each sample and rest as much as possible between samples.

When you taste, first of all smell each sample, then rest and record your impressions of each beer as you go. Always remember to trust your first instincts. Repeat the exercise and add to your score card if necessary. Now taste and do the same. Most beer tasters swallow the product rather than expectorating. I prefer to swallow the beer because it assures the beer reaches the back of the throat where the bitter detectors are mostly located. However, some stouts have extreme flavor impacts and, if these are included, it may be fine to expectorate and rinse or chew between samples. As you smell and taste, keep in mind the scorecard. Your impressions of the beers are confined by the scorecard as well as expressed through it, and you must use it wisely.

The score card is an important device for any tasting, including your private and personal tastings of beers. It is the record of what is experienced, and in serious work, is the source of data that might even be published (for example, figure 4.2 in this chapter). The most common type of tasting is a descriptive analysis, meaning the taster is creating a flavor profile. The scorecard for this purpose provides a familiar list of aroma, taste, and mouthfeel qualities (a lexicon of terms or descriptors) and a means of quantifying them, usually on a five-, seven-, or nine-point scale. The scales are often "anchored" with words like "none" (value one, on the scale) and "extreme" (value nine, on the scale). The descriptive words themselves are, for the most part, well understood by all the tasters, who use them fairly consistently. The score card might have all the words on the well-known ASBC flavor wheel or on the AHA list (table 4.5) or a subset of them that particularly suits the project or products in hand. Regardless of the length of the list of terms provided, you will probably use only some of the descriptors consistently. Our limited list of descriptors at the beginning of this chapter (table 4.1) is a good example of selection of descriptive terms. If the number of descriptors and beers is few, the data of your panel can be conveniently displayed as a spiderweb plot, as shown in figures 4.3 and 4.4. Not all tasting is done this way.

In chapter 2, I quote Michael Jackson's extraordinary description of his reaction to imperial stouts. What is important about Jackson's kind of flavor analysis is that it is intensely personal. It draws not upon a lexicon of words that might be well understood and used in some consistent way by a group of tasters, but instead on a lexicon drawn from an individual's memory as modified by experience and fancy. There is, therefore, some passionate or emotional or evocative connection between the product and the taster who is given free and creative rein. Thus, the place where the tasting takes place, the companions, the history and fame of the product, whether tasted with food or not, and recollections from past experiences of that product all contribute to this personal evaluation. It might be important for you as an individual to engage in this kind of tasting and to draw connections between the flavor impacts of the product you are tasting and your own flavor and aroma memory and experience. Thus, if you first tasted Guinness in a crowded, noisy, smoky, London pub with the first love of your life wearing a heady cologne, there is nothing wrong with evoking those memories in your personal evaluation of stouts when at home. Indeed, it is a special delight! It's just important to recognize that this is not a descriptive analysis or a flavor profile, that it is non-quantitative and heavily confounded or biased data and, therefore, that your impressions gained in this way are highly valuable to you only, and irrelevant to others who have a completely different flavor memory and set of experiences.

I know of beer drinkers who keep extensive logs of the beers they taste with intricate descriptions of their reactions to the products. They never forget a single beer they taste. Several publications which cater to this hobby provide interesting tour guides to beer regions, taste and analytical profiles of the beers and score cards to record the traveler's own impressions. This reminds me a bit of bird watching where one tracks down a bird in its natural habitat and, having seen it, checks it off the list. I think this is a fascinating hobby, and I'm delighted that so many enjoy it so much, but it is not my hobby. Unlike birds, beers change from time to time and place to place, and even — especially in craft-brewed American beers or those that have traveled a long way to get here — bottle to bottle. Certainly, I change from time to time, and so my impressions of beers are not constant. What I enjoyed today might be tomorrow's also-ran. When asked, "What is your favorite beer?" I generally reply, "What have you got?" and taste and enjoy it for the moment.

5

Our Survey
of Stout Brewers

We wrote to all the stout brewers we could identify
anywhere in the world advising them about this monograph and seeking information suitable for publication in
it. The idea was (1) to get a cross-section of stout brewing
practices worldwide, (2) to gauge the extent to which
these practices might be uniquely different from another
comparable brewing practice (such as generic ale), and (3)
to measure whether and how stout brewing differs from
the other products of each brewery that makes stout. As
expected, we did not get replies from every brewer; in
fact relatively few responded. We sincerely thank those
brewers who did reply and who shared with us the details
of their processes. We are especially grateful to those
brewers who sent us samples of their product for inclusion in our analyses and for flavor evaluation.

Brewers answered the questions we asked in many
different ways. While I have slightly edited the material
for the convenience of the reader, I have left the
responses almost entirely as we received them. Some of
the answers are ambiguous, as perhaps some of the questions are, but I have not second-guessed the intent of the

brewers' answers. Though, in retrospect, some questions we asked are a bit unnecessary, here they are:

SURVEY RESPONSES

Castle Milk Stout, South African Breweries

Production

Volume of beer produced per year by your brewery?
4.1 million hL/year

Volume of stout produced per year?
92,400 hL/year

Brew length for stout?
739 hL

Raw Materials

What is composition of brewing water used for stouts?
Dechlorinated mains water ex-municipality

If water is specifically treated for stout production, how is it treated?
Not treated

Is this water different from that used for your other beers?
Not different

Choice barley grain is slow roasted to produce a rich, dark brew. A unique blend of hops adds a touch of bitterness, and a special yeast fixes the unmistakable flavour and creamy head.

SAB

6% alc/vol   375 ml

Stout

What types of specialty malts, roasted products, and/or adjuncts are used?
10% black (roasted malt) and 35% maltose syrup

Do you have a preferred type of pale malt for stout brewing?
No

Do you use a special yeast strain to produce your stout?
No

What pitching rate do you use for stout worts?
1.3 kg/hL wort

Do you use special yeast handling techniques (skimming, washing)?
No

What form of hops do you use for stout brewing?
Pellets and extract

What hop varieties?
George Southern Brewer (local South African pellets)

What hop varieties do you use for bitterness?
34 kg pellets and 11 kg extract

If you use aroma hops, what method of addition is used?
Kettle hopping

Mashing Practices

Milling practices (multi-roll, wet milling, etc.)?
Steep conditioned milling

Mash temperature(s)?
118°/143°/158°/168°F (48°/62°/70°/76°C) profile

Grist to water ratio?
38 kg malt per hL water

Mash separation practice (lauter, mash filter, etc.)?
Lauter tun

Kettle Boiling

If finings are added to the kettle what type(s) do you use?
No kettle finings

Is your kettle directly or indirectly heated?
Indirectly heated

If indirect, internal or external calandria?
Internal calandria

What is the length of time of your boil?
90-minute boil

Is color/flavor pick-up at this stage important to you?
Yes, flavor pick-up

Fermentation and Conditioning

What fermenter design do you use for stout?
Cylindroconical

What is the temperature and duration of your stout fermentation?
6 days at 53°F (12°C), then chilled to 36°F (2.5°C)

How is your yeast harvested for repitching?
Yeast not repitched, scrapped after 5 days

What method(s) do you use to clarify your stout?
Collagen finings in storage

Do you use any special techniques for flavor maturation?
No

How do you carbonate your stout?
Carbonate on transfer from FV to SV (storage vessel)

Package and Dispense

What types of packages do you use for stout?
Packages are 340 and 450 mL cans, 375 mL pints, 745 mL quarts

If available in kegs, what dispense method is used?
No kegs

Physical and Chemical Analysis

Original Gravity (°Plato)
1.057 (14.3 °Plato)

Alcohol by weight (volume)
6% (7.5%)

Bitterness (IBU)
29 (±2)

Color SRM (EBC)
76 (±11) (200 [±30] EBC)

Carbon dioxide
2.5 (±0.15) vol.

Volume of other gases
Air max 0.2%

Other important analytical attributes you would like to include.
Diacetyl 75 (±15) ug/dm^3

If you have a standard in-house flavor profile please include it.
Sweetness–5; bitterness–7; body–7; ester–1; caramel–3; astringency–2

Miscellaneous Information
Brewed since 1984; not in United States. A sweet stout, our product is a blend between bitter and sweet. The "perceived sweetness" comes from high diacetyl levels and a certain acrid flavor from black malt.

Stallion Stout,
Banks Breweries Ltd., Barbados

Production

Volume of beer produced per year by your brewery?
    100,000 U.S. bbl./year

Volume of stout produced per year?
    7,500 U.S. bbl./year

Brew length for stout?
    95 U.S. bbl.

Raw Materials

What is composition of brewing water used for stouts?
    Hardness 150 ppm $CaCO_3$; Alkalinity 1.0–0.5

If water is specifically treated for stout production, how is it treated?
    Lime softened

Is this water different from that used for your other beers?
    Yes

What types of specialty malts, roasted products, and/or adjuncts are used?
    CaraPils and roasted barley

Do you have a preferred type of pale malt for stout brewing?
    Two-row Pilsen

Do you use a special yeast strain to produce your stout?
    Yes

What pitching rate do you use for stout worts?
    16 to 18 x 10^6 cells/mL

Do you use special yeast handling techniques (skimming, washing)?
    No

What hop varieties do you use for bitterness?
    U.S.

What hop varieties do you use for aroma?
    European

If you use aroma hops, what method of addition is used?
    Kettle addition

Mashing Practices

Milling practices (multi-roll, wet milling, etc.)?
    Dry multi-roll mill

Mash temperature(s)?
    155°F (68°C)

Grist to water ratio?
   1:3.3

Mash separation practice (lauter, mash filter, etc.)?
   Lauter

Kettle Boiling

If finings are added to the kettle what type(s) do you use?
   No kettle finings

Is your kettle directly or indirectly heated?
   Directly heated

What is the length of time of your boil?
   80-minute boil

Is color/flavor pick-up at this stage important to you?
   Color/flavor pick-up is important

Fermentation and Conditioning

What fermenter design do you use for stout?
   Cylindroconical vessels

What is the temperature and duration of your stout fermentation?
   10 days fermentation

How is your yeast harvested for repitching?
   Yeast not harvested for repitching

What method(s) do you use to clarify your stout?
   Cooling, cold finings, and filtration

Stout

Do you use any special techniques for flavor maturation?
No

How do you carbonate your stout?
Carbonate by injection

Package and Dispense

What types of packages do you use for stout?
Bottle only

Physical and Chemical Analysis

Original Gravity (°Plato)
1.068 (17 °Plato)

Real and/or apparent extract
1.015 (3.8 °Plato)

Bitterness (IBU)
21

Color SRM (EBC)
129 (340 EBC)

Carbon dioxide
2.5 vol.

Volume of other gases
less than 1

If you have a standard in-house flavor profile please include it.
Fresh; caramel; hoppy; very estery; spicy; alcoholic; sweet

Miscellaneous Information
Dry stout is dark, hoppy, average bodied, slightly acid, alcoholic, slightly astringent, coffeelike. Sweet stout is sweet, estery, more body than dry stout, dark colored malty, coffeelike. Balanced hoppiness, caramel, alcoholic.

Sheaf Stout, Carlton and United Breweries, Australia

Production

Volume of beer produced per year by your brewery?
3 million hL total

Volume of stout produced per year?
16,000 hL

Brew length for stout?
770 hL

Raw Materials

What is composition of brewing water used for stouts?
Composition, mg/L: Total hardness (as $CaCO_3$) 30; Ca^{++} 10; Na^+ 20; Cl^- 50; SO_4^- 50; Ca^{++} salts added to the mash 50 mg/L

If water is specifically treated for stout production, how is it treated?
Sand- and carbon-filtered town's water

Is this water different from that used for your other beers?
Not different

What types of specialty malts, roasted products, and/or adjuncts are used?
Lager malt; crystal malt; roasted barley; maltose syrup

Do you have a preferred type of pale malt for stout brewing?
No

Do you use a special yeast strain to produce your stout?
A top-fermenting ale yeast

What pitching rate do you use for stout worts?
10 million cells/mL

Do you use special yeast handling techniques (skimming, washing)?
No

What form of hops do you use for stout brewing?
Hop pellets

What hop varieties do you use for bitterness?
Pride of Ringwood 50 kg/brew

Mashing Practices

Milling practices (multi-roll, wet milling, etc.)?
Six-roll dry mill

Mash separation practice (lauter, mash filter, etc.)?
Lauter tun

Kettle Boiling

Is your kettle directly or indirectly heated?
Kettle directly heated

What is the length of time of your boil?
90-minute boil

Is color/flavor pick-up at this stage important to you?
Important for bitterness

Fermentation and Conditioning

What fermenter design do you use for stout?
Cylindroconical fermenters

How is your yeast harvested for repitching?
Yeast not repitched

What method(s) do you use to clarify your stout?
Minimum of 2 weeks storage at 32°F (0°C), centrifuge, then DE filter

How do you carbonate your stout?
Carbonated in line

Package and Dispense

What types of packages do you use for stout?
350 mL and 750 mL bottles

Physical and Chemical Analysis

Original Gravity (°Plato)
1.056 (14.1 °Plato)

Real and/or apparent extract
1.015 (3.7 °Plato)

Alcohol by weight (volume)
4.5% (5.7%)

Bitterness (IBU)
35

Color SRM (EBC)
80 (210 EBC)

Carbon dioxide
0.51%

If you have a standard in-house flavor profile please include it.
Full-bodied with pleasant fruity, mild roasted coffee aroma with clean hop bitterness and roasted flavors on the palate.

Miscellaneous Information
    History: Stout has been brewed for many years by this company since at least 1926. That includes Bull Stout and White Horse Stout (neither are now brewed) as well as Sheaf Stout, which is currently brewed for local and export consumption in the United States.

Carbine Stout, Castlemaine Perkins Ltd., Queensland, Australia

Production

Volume of beer produced per year by your brewery?
    2,500,000 hL

Volume of stout produced per year?
    7,500 hL

Brew length for stout?
    380 hL

Raw Materials

What is composition of brewing water used for stouts?
    Local authority water

If water is specifically treated for stout production, how is it treated?
    Salts added to increase Ca^{++} to 300 ppm and Mg^{++} to 12 ppm

Stout

Is this water different from that used for your other beers?
Not different

What types of specialty malts, roasted products, and/or adjuncts are used?
Roasted malt

Do you have a preferred type of pale malt for stout brewing?
No

Do you use a special yeast strain to produce your stout?
No

What pitching rate do you use for stout worts?
20×10^6 cells/mL

Do you use special yeast handling techniques (skimming, washing)?
Yeast washed at pH 2 to 2.3 for 1 hour using sulphuric acid

What form of hops do you use for stout brewing?
Cone hops

What hop varieties do you use for bitterness?
Pride of Ringwood approximately 60 kg

What hop varieties do you use for aroma?
Golden Cluster approximately 20 kg

If you use aroma hops, what method of addition is used?
Kettle addition

Mashing Practices

Milling practices (multi-roll, wet milling, etc.)?
Multi-roll dry milling

Mash temperature(s)?
158°F (70°C)

Grist to water ratio?
1:3.3

Mash separation practice (lauter, mash filter, etc.)?
Lauter tun

Kettle Boiling

If finings are added to the kettle what type(s) do you use?
No kettle finings

Is your kettle directly or indirectly heated?
Indirectly heated

If indirect, internal or external calandria?
Internal calandria

What is the length of time of your boil?
Boil for 90 minutes

Is color/flavor pick-up at this stage important to you?
Color/flavor pick-up important

Fermentation and Conditioning

What fermenter design do you use for stout?
Fermenters 2,500 hL vertical stainless steel

What is the temperature and duration of your stout fermentation?
Pitching temperature 46°F (8°C) rising to 65°F (18°C); 4-day duration

How is your yeast harvested for repitching?
Stout yeast not repitched

What method(s) do you use to clarify your stout?
Clarify by isinglass finings and filtration

Do you use any special techniques for flavor maturation?
No

How do you carbonate your stout?
Carbonate by Witteman carbonator

Package and Dispense

What types of packages do you use for stout?
Bottles

Physical and Chemical Analysis

Original Gravity (°Plato)
1.052 (13 °Plato)

Real and/or apparent extract
1.011 (2.8 °Plato)

Alcohol by weight (volume)
4.1% (5.1%)

Bitterness (IBU)
41

Color SRM (EBC)
55 (145 EBC)

Carbon dioxide
0.53%

Volume of other gases
0.7 mL per 375 mL bottle

Miscellaneous Information
Castlemaine XXXX lager beer available in Hawaii through Paradise Beverages, Honolulu

Dragon Stout, Desnoes and Geddes Ltd., Kingston, Jamaica W.I.

Production

Volume of beer produced per year by your brewery?
750,000 bbl.

Volume of stout produced per year?
200,000 bbl.

Brew length for stout?
5 x 600 bbl./24 hr.

Raw Materials

What is composition of brewing water used for stouts?
Hardness 100 ppm as Ca^{++} (gypsum treated). Alkalinity 50 ppm as $CaCO_3$; pH 8-10; Chloride 200 ppm as Cl^-

If water is specifically treated for stout production, how is it treated?
Cold lime treated

Is this water different from that used for your other beers?
Not different; as of November 1993, all brewing water treated by reverse osmosis

What types of specialty malts, roasted products, and/or adjuncts are used?
Black malt, caramel malt, caramel coloring, brewing corn syrup

Do you have a preferred type of pale malt for stout brewing?
Six-row malt for high DP and lauter efficiency

Do you use a special yeast strain to produce your stout?
Our own lager yeast

What pitching rate do you use for stout worts?
Pitching rate 20 x 10^6 cells/mL

Do you use special yeast handling techniques (skimming, washing)?
We occasionally acid-treat our yeast

What form of hops do you use for stout brewing?
Extract

What hop varieties do you use for bitterness?
Extract to deliver 30 BUs in the finished product

Mashing Practices

Milling practices (multi-roll, wet milling, etc.)?
Dry milling, six-roll mill

Mash temperature(s)?
40-minute boil at 120°F (49°C); heat to 136°F (58°C) rest 10 minutes; cooker contents transferred to 155°F (68°C); raise to 172°F (78°C) before transfer to lauter

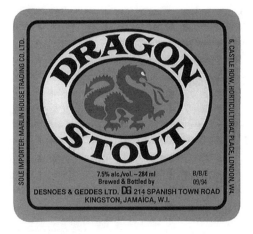

Grist to water ratio?
 1.5 bbl. water to 100 lb. material or combined mash (nearly 4:1)

Mash separation practice (lauter, mash filter, etc.)?
 Lauter

Kettle Boiling

If finings are added to the kettle what type(s) do you use?
 Kettle finings marine algae

Is your kettle directly or indirectly heated?
 Indirectly heated

If indirect, internal or external calandria?
 Internal calandria

What is the length of time of your boil?
 Boil for 60 minutes prior to full, 60 minutes after (total 2 hours)

Is color/flavor pick-up at this stage important to you?
 Color/flavor pick-up is not important

Fermentation and Conditioning

What fermenter design do you use for stout?
 Horizontal cylindrical

What is the temperature and duration of your stout fermentation?
 Pitching temperature 59°F (15°C), fermenting 70°F (21°C), duration
 120 hours

How is your yeast harvested for repitching?
 Yeast harvested by paddle to tank outlet, pump to yeast room, screened
 into weigh brinks

Stout

What method(s) do you use to clarify your stout?
Clarify by isinglass finings in storage

Do you use any special techniques for flavor maturation?
Our franchise stout employs a special beer flavoring extract

How do you carbonate your stout?
Carbonate by pinpoint carbonation

Package and Dispense

What types of packages do you use for stout?
Bottles

Physical and Chemical Analysis

Original Gravity (°Plato)
1.074 (18.4 °Plato)

Real and/or apparent extract
1.018 (4.5 °Plato)

Alcohol by weight (volume)
6% (7.5%)

Bitterness (IBU)
30

Color SRM (EBC)
76 (200 EBC)

Carbon dioxide
2.6 vol.

If you have a standard in-house flavor profile please include it.
A pleasant bitter/sweet/alcohol balance

Miscellaneous Information
Imported by Labatts. Dry stout is fully attenuated, ABV at least 7% and no priming sugar. In sweet stout, priming sugar used on way to bottling tanks, providing both body and sweetness.

Kirin Stout, Kirin Brewery Co., Kyoto Plant, Japan

Production

Volume of beer produced per year by your brewery?
2.1 million bbl. (3 million hL)/year

Volume of stout produced per year?
430 bbl. (600 hL)/year

Raw Materials

What is composition of brewing water used for stouts?
Drinking water supplied by our city

If water is specifically treated for stout production, how is it treated?
Treatment nothing particular

Is this water different from that used for your other beers?
No (same)

What types of specialty malts, roasted products, and/or adjuncts are used?
Crystal malt; strong-colored malt (farb malt); adjuncts — rice, sugar

Do you have a preferred type of pale malt for stout brewing?
No preferred type of pale malt

Do you use a special yeast strain to produce your stout?
Yeast originated from U.K. for stout

What pitching rate do you use for stout worts?
0.4% (liters centrifuged pressed yeast per liter of wort)

Do you use special yeast handling techniques (skimming, washing)?
If we have to store harvested yeast for a long time we activate it by aeration before next pitching

What form of hops do you use for stout brewing?
Dried cone hops and pellets

What hop varieties do you use for bitterness?
30% of total amount German bitter hop

What hop varieties do you use for aroma?
70% of total amount Bohemian fine aroma hop

If you use aroma hops, what method of addition is used?
Kettle addition of all hops

Mashing Practices

Milling practices (multi-roll, wet milling, etc.)?
Pale malt multi-roll mill (wet conditioning), dark malt dry milled

Mash temperature(s)?
Infusion program 140–158°F (60–70°C) is adopted

Grist to water ratio?
Approximately 250 kg grist/kL mash (4:1)

Mash separation practice (lauter, mash filter, etc.)?
Lauter

Kettle Boiling

If finings are added to the kettle what type(s) do you use?
Finings are not used

Is your kettle directly or indirectly heated?
Indirectly heated by steam

If indirect, internal or external calandria?
Multi-pipe system internal calandria

What is the length of time of your boil?
Boil for 120 minutes

Is color/flavor pick-up at this stage important to you?
Color/flavor pick-up usually checked when boiling is finished

Fermentation and Conditioning

What fermenter design do you use for stout?
Cylindroconical vessels used

What is the temperature and duration of your stout fermentation?
Fermenting temperature 53–60°F (12–16°C)

How is your yeast harvested for repitching?
Harvested by yeast separator (centrifuge)

What method(s) do you use to clarify your stout?
Centrifuge and kieselguhr filtration

Do you use any special techniques for flavor maturation?
Nothing particular

How do you carbonate your stout?
We adjust CO_2 content during filtration process

Package and Dispense

What types of packages do you use for stout?
Bottle (334 mL) and keg (7 L)

If available in kegs, what dispense method is used?
CO_2 gas is used for charging pressure into keg

Physical and Chemical Analysis

Real and/or apparent extract
    1.014 (3.5 °Plato)

Alcohol by weight (volume)
    6.4% (8%)

Bitterness (IBU)
    40

Color SRM (EBC)
    102 (270 EBC)

Carbon dioxide
    0.47%

Other important analytical attributes you would like to include.
    Much higher concentration of ester component and phenolic component than our regular lager-type beer

If you have a standard in-house flavor profile please include it.
    Sharp; bitter; estery; (caramel) malt flavor; sour

Miscellaneous Information
    We started producing stout in 1932 and added minor changes in the brewing process for brewing "real English-type" stout in later 1980s. Our stout may be compared to our black beer: Alcohol: 8% vs. 5%; Color: 270 vs. 100 EBC; Character: more vs. less estery and more vs. less bitter.

Beamish Stout and Beamish Genuine Stout, Beamish and Crawford PLC, Cork, Ireland

Production

Volume of beer produced per year by your brewery?
    360,000 (36 gal. bbl.)

Volume of stout produced per year?
    216,000 bbl.

Brew length for stout?
    4.5 hr., 225 bbl. brew size

Raw Materials

What is composition of brewing water used for stouts?
    Fully demineralized and filtered through activated carbon

If water is specifically treated for stout production, how is it treated?
    Water, apart from salts addition, is the same

Is this water different from that used for your other beers?
    Different amount of salts addition

Stout

What types of specialty malts, roasted products, and/or adjuncts are used?
Ale malt, roast barley

Do you have a preferred type of pale malt for stout brewing?
Blenharm malt; Juliet barley for roast

Do you use a special yeast strain to produce your stout?
Yes; special yeast strain evolved from the original ale yeast

What pitching rate do you use for stout worts?
6–8 x 10^6 cells/mL

Do you use special yeast handling techniques (skimming, washing)?
Acid washing

What form of hops do you use for stout brewing?
Pellet hops

What hop varieties do you use for bitterness?
Target/Challenger/Perle

What hop varieties do you use for aroma?
Challenger/Goldings

If you use aroma hops, what method of addition is used?
Kettle addition

Mashing Practices

Mash temperature(s)?
143°F (62°C) for 45 minutes

Grist to water ratio?
3.5:1

Mash separation practice (lauter, mash filter, etc.)?
Lauter tun

Kettle Boiling

If finings are added to the kettle what type(s) do you use?
Kettle finings Atlanta flock (Carrageenan)

Is your kettle directly or indirectly heated?
Indirectly heated

What is the length of time of your boil?
Boil for 90 minutes

Is color/flavor pick-up at this stage important to you?
Color/flavor pick-up important

Fermentation and Conditioning

What fermenter design do you use for stout?
Cylindroconical fermenters

What is the temperature and duration of your stout fermentation?
73°F (22°C) for 75-hour duration

How is your yeast harvested for repitching?
Cropped from bottom of fermenter

What method(s) do you use to clarify your stout?
Clarify by finings in fermentation vessel

Do you use any special techniques for flavor maturation?
No

How do you carbonate your stout?
In tank carbonation (for bottling only)

Package and Dispense

What types of packages do you use for stout?
All package types

If available in kegs, what dispense method is used?
Yes; mixed gas 30/70% mixture

Physical and Chemical Analysis

Original Gravity (°Plato)
1.038 (9.5 °Plato)

Alcohol by weight (volume)
5.2–5.3% (4.1–4.2%)

Bitterness (IBU)
38–40

Color SRM (EBC)
46–53 (120–140 EBC)

Carbon dioxide
1.15 vol.

Volume of other gases
60 ppm

Other important analytical attributes you would like to include.
Distinctive roastiness

Miscellaneous Information
We use on line nitrogenization. Established since 1792; oldest stout brewery. Available in Boston and Atlanta.

ABC Extra Stout and Guinness Foreign Extra Stout, Asia-Pacific Breweries, Singapore

Production:

Volume of beer produced per year by your brewery?
  1,000,000 hL/year

Volume of stout produced per year?
  140,000 hL/year

Brew length for stout?
  We can do about 200,000 hL/year

Raw Materials

What is composition of brewing water used for stouts?
  · Standard drinking water quality, pH 5.7, hardness about 6°G

If water is specifically treated for stout production, how is it treated?
  We add $CaCl_2$ to adjust hardness

Is this water different from that used for your other beers?
  Water the same as other beers

What types of specialty malts, roasted products, and/or adjuncts are used?
  Pale malt, roasted barley, sugar

Do you have a preferred type of pale malt for stout brewing?
  No

Do you use a special yeast strain to produce your stout?
  Yes, special yeast strain used

What pitching rate do you use for stout worts?
0.6 kg yeast/hL (60% consistency)

Do you use special yeast handling techniques (skimming, washing)?
No

What form of hops do you use for stout brewing?
Extract

What hop varieties do you use for bitterness?
11 kg a-acid/360 hL

What hop varieties do you use for aroma?
No

Mashing Practices

Milling practices (multi-roll, wet milling, etc.)?
Six-roller mill

Mash temperature(s)?
145°F (63°C)

Grist to water ratio?
3:1

Mash separation practice (lauter, mash filter, etc.)?
Lauter tun

Kettle Boiling

Is your kettle directly or indirectly heated?
Indirectly heated

If indirect, internal or external calandria?
External

What is the length of time of your boil?
Boil for 90 minutes

Is color/flavor pick-up at this stage important to you?
Color/flavor pick-up not important

Fermentation and Conditioning

What fermenter design do you use for stout?
Cylindroconical fermenters

What is the temperature and duration of your stout fermentation?
Fermentation temperature 71–75°F (22–24°C)

How is your yeast harvested for repitching?
Gyle or fresh

What method(s) do you use to clarify your stout?
Clarify by centrifugation

Do you use any special techniques for flavor maturation?
No special techniques for flavor maturation

Stout

How do you carbonate your stout?
> Pin-point carbonator

Package and Dispense

What types of packages do you use for stout?
> Cans and bottles

Physical and Chemical Analysis

Original Gravity (°Plato)
> 1.070 (17.5 °Plato)

Real and/or apparent extract
> 1.012 (3 °Plato)

Alcohol by weight (volume)
> 6% (7.5%)

Bitterness (IBU)
> 60

Color SRM (EBC)
> 61–91 (160–240 EBC)

Carbon dioxide
> 0.50%

If you have a standard in-house flavor profile please include it.
> We brew a strong stout with a typically roasted flavor.

Miscellaneous Information
> No special brewing techniques.

Moss Bay Stout, Hales Ales, Kirkland and Spokane, Washington

Production

Volume of beer produced per year by your brewery?
> 8K

Volume of stout produced per year?
> 350 bbl.

Brew length for stout?
> 10 bbl.

Raw Materials

What is composition of brewing water used for stouts?
> Soft (low mineral)

If water is specifically treated for stout production, how is it treated?
No (gypsum)

Is this water different from that used for your other beers?
Not different

What types of specialty malts, roasted products, and/or adjuncts are used?
Carastan, crystal, dark crystal, black

Do you have a preferred type of pale malt for stout brewing?
No

Do you use a special yeast strain to produce your stout?
No

What pitching rate do you use for stout worts?
1lb./100 gal.

Do you use special yeast handling techniques (skimming, washing)?
No

What form of hops do you use for stout brewing?
Pellets, cones

What hop varieties do you use for bitterness?
Clusters

What hop varieties do you use for aroma?
Hallertauer

If you use aroma hops, what method of addition is used?
Kettle addition

Mashing Practices

Milling practices (multi-roll, wet milling, etc.)?
Single roller, dry mill

Mash temperature(s)?
152°F (67°C)

Kettle Boiling

Is your kettle directly or indirectly heated?
Directly heated

What is the length of time of your boil?
Boil for 60 minutes

Is color/flavor pick-up at this stage important to you?
Color/flavor pick-up is important

Fermentation and Conditioning

What is the temperature and duration of your stout fermentation?
Fermentation temperature 68°F (20°C) for 96-hour duration

How is your yeast harvested for repitching?
Skimming

111

Stout

What method(s) do you use to clarify your stout?
Leaf filtration

Do you use any special techniques for flavor maturation?
No

How do you carbonate your stout?
Carbonation by injection

Package and Dispense

What types of packages do you use for stout?
Keg

If available in kegs, what dispense method is used?
Nitrogen/CO_2, 75/25% mixture

Physical and Chemical Analysis

Original Gravity (°Plato)
1.054 (13.5 °Plato)

Miscellaneous Information
Dry stout is roasted, blackish, dry, hoppy. Sweet stout is malty, smooth, semi-sweet, round, creamy. Stouts are blacker, bigger, fuller than other black beers.

San Quentin's Breakout Stout, Marin Brewing Co., Larkspur, California

Production

Volume of beer produced per year by your brewery?
2,004 bbl.

Volume of stout produced per year?
121 bbl.

Brew length for stout?
14 bbl.

Raw Materials

What is composition of brewing water used for stouts?
Data provided from Marin Municipal Water District: pH 6.9–8.2; Calcium 11–19 mg/L; total hardness 60–86 mg/L; total dissolved solids 91–140; magnesium 6–10 mg/L

If water is specifically treated for stout production, how is it treated?
Not treated

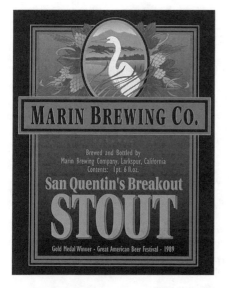

Is this water different from that used for your other beers?
Not different

What types of specialty malts, roasted products, and/or adjuncts are used?
Roasted barley, black patent malt, wheat malt

Do you have a preferred type of pale malt for stout brewing?
Great Western pale

Do you use a special yeast strain to produce your stout?
Same yeast for all beers is Wyeast #1056

Do you use special yeast handling techniques (skimming, washing)?
No

What form of hops do you use for stout brewing?
Pellets

What hop varieties do you use for bitterness?
Centennial usually — can vary

What hop varieties do you use for aroma?
None

Mashing Practices

Milling practices (multi-roll, wet milling, etc.)?
Two-roll mill

Mash temperature(s)?
158°F (70°C)

Grist to water ratio?
Not measured — mash is quite stiff

113

Kettle Boiling

If finings are added to the kettle what type(s) do you use?
No kettle finings

Is your kettle directly or indirectly heated?
Directly heated by gas flame

What is the length of time of your boil?
Boil for 60 minutes

Is color/flavor pick-up at this stage important to you?
Color/flavor pick-up is not important

Fermentation and Conditioning

What fermenter design do you use for stout?
Unitank

What is the temperature and duration of your stout fermentation?
71–72°F (22°C) 3 days duration

How is your yeast harvested for repitching?
Pushed from cone to cone (of fermenters) with CO_2

What method(s) do you use to clarify your stout?
No clarification (settlement) — not filtered

Do you use any special techniques for flavor maturation?
No

How do you carbonate your stout?
Carbonation by top pressure in unitank; 16–17 psig 7 days at 35°F (2°C)

Package and Dispense

What types of packages do you use for stout?
22-oz. bottles and 5-gal. kegs at the brewery only

If available in kegs, what dispense method is used?
Dispense by CO_2 or a hand pump

Physical and Chemical Analysis

Original Gravity (°Plato)
1.064 (16 °Plato)

Real and/or apparent extract
1.020 (5 °Plato)

Alcohol by weight (volume)
4.7% (5.9%)

Bitterness (IBU)
35

Color SRM (EBC)
    35–40 (92–105 EBC)

Carbon dioxide
    2.2–2.3 vol.

Miscellaneous Information
    Our stout is quite strong in alcohol. Sweet stouts are black, moderate roasted barley aroma and flavor, moderate hopping with a pronounced sweetness. Caramel malts often used. Imperial stout has very high alcohol, strong roasted barley aroma and flavor, well hopped (bittered only), and rather dry. Estery, alcoholic nose too.

XXXXX Stout, Pike Place Brewery, Seattle, Washington

Production

Volume of beer produced per year by your brewery?
    2,000 bbl./year

Volume of stout produced per year?
    70+ bbl./year

Brew length for stout?
    4.5 bbl. (9-bbl. fermenters)

Raw Materials

What is composition of brewing water used for stouts?
    Seattle City water plus 6 oz. of gypsum for 9 bbl. of stout

If water is specifically treated for stout production, how is it treated?
    Slightly more gypsum than other beers

Is this water different from that used for your other beers?
    Not different

What types of specialty malts, roasted products, and/or adjuncts are used?
    Roasted barley from crisp malting (U.K.)

Do you have a preferred type of pale malt for stout brewing?
    Pale malt Maris Otter two-row (U.K.)

Do you use a special yeast strain to produce your stout?
    Yeast is the same "London" strain used in all our beers

What pitching rate do you use for stout worts?
    Pitching rate 1 million cells/mL/°Plato (slightly higher than pale ale)

Do you use special yeast handling techniques (skimming, washing)?
    No

What form of hops do you use for stout brewing?
Cone hops

What hop varieties do you use for bitterness?
Chinook or other high a-acid hop 60 BUs

What hop varieties do you use for aroma?
Kent Goldings

If you use aroma hops, what method of addition is used?
Late kettle addition

Mashing Practices

Milling practices (multi-roll, wet milling, etc.)?
Two-roll dry mill

Mash temperature(s)?
150–152°F (66–67°C)

Grist to water ratio?
Thick mash

Mash separation practice (lauter, mash filter, etc.)?
Mash/lauter tun (one vessel)

Kettle Boiling

If finings are added to the kettle what type(s) do you use?
Irish moss (6 oz. for 9 bbl.)

Is your kettle directly or indirectly heated?
Directly heated by electric elements

What is the length of time of your boil?
Boil for 90 minutes

Is color/flavor pick-up at this stage important to you?
Color/flavor pick-up is important

Fermentation and Conditioning

What fermenter design do you use for stout?
Cylindroconical

What is the temperature and duration of your stout fermentation?
72–74°F (22–23°C) for 48–60 hours duration

How is your yeast harvested for repitching?
Drawn from bottom of conical fermenter

What method(s) do you use to clarify your stout?
No clarification (settlement)

Do you use any special techniques for flavor maturation?
5–7 weeks of cold (40–45°F [4–7°C]) storage for flavor maturation

Package and Dispense

What types of packages do you use for stout?
   keg mostly; a few 22-oz. bottles

If available in kegs, what dispense method is used?
   CO_2 or N_2/CO_2 mixture depending on distance to the bar

Physical and Chemical Analysis

Original Gravity (°Plato)
   1.070–1.072 (17.5–18 °Plato)

Real and/or apparent extract
   1.023 (5.7 °Plato)

Alcohol by weight (volume)
   4.4% (5.5%)

Bitterness (IBU)
   60

Color SRM (EBC)
   Black to very dark

Carbon dioxide
   2.6–2.7 vol.

Miscellaneous Information
   The 5–7 weeks of aging gives the stout mellowness and a tight dark brown head. Our beer is rather large for the Dublin dry style and some may consider it too big for that style, although we don't.

To complete this survey we analyzed our experimental beers and the stouts used in our tasting. For this we thank our friends, especially Jim Wilson, at the Anheuser-Busch Company in Fairfield, California, whose SCABA machine soon made short work of our samples. Not much comment is required about the data, but for those who find fascination in real data here is enough to keep you busy for a while.

Table 5.1 lists our experimental beers made with different waters. Water "A" ("ale" type) is most acidifying or least alkalizing, and water "C" is least acidifying or most alkalizing. The original gravity (OG expressed in the table as degrees Plato), and therefore the alcohol level, is low because the beers were designed to test the effects of water

TABLE 5.1

Roast Barley	Water Used	SG	OG (°Plato)	ABW %	RE %	RDF %	AE %	ADF %	ABV %	Kilo-Calories	Color	pH
7%	A	1.01085	9.78	2.88	4.12	59.16	2.78	71.600	3.69	129.10	47.04	3.89
	B	1.00747	9.54	3.14	3.37	65.83	1.91	79.900	4.00	124.30	47.74	4.04
	C	1.00727	9.36	3.09	3.30	65.93	1.87	80.100	3.93	121.80	48.88	4.19
9%	A	1.00885	9.97	3.18	3.74	63.70	2.27	77.200	4.05	130.70	52.12	3.87
	B	1.00550	8.97	3.10	2.85	69.23	1.41	84.200	3.95	115.70	52.78	4.01
	C	1.00756	9.84	3.26	3.45	66.14	1.94	80.300	4.15	128.30	54.78	4.21
11%	A	1.00796	9.33	3.00	3.43	64.35	2.04	78.100	3.82	121.70	56.90	3.96
	B	1.00758	9.57	3.14	3.40	65.63	1.94	79.700	4.00	124.80	57.51	4.17
	C	1.00932	9.55	2.95	3.75	61.86	2.39	75.000	3.76	125.30	57.41	4.25

Water A — Deionized water plus CaSO$_4$ (gypsum).
Water B — Deionized water only.
Water C — Deionized water plus mixed salts = Dublin water.

composition and roasted material on stout flavor and analysis. This is most easily detected if the beers are relatively low gravity. The more alkaline water (water "C") increased stout pH (less acidity) and color, but there was no consistent affect on beer specific gravity; real extract (RE); real (RDF) or apparent (ADF) degree of fermentation; nor on content of alcohol or calories. Water with a higher potential alkalinity (as previously noted) increased perceived bitterness and roasty flavor.

The data on commercial stouts serve to support the view that there is no single interpretation of the word "stout." The analytical parameters shown here, with the obvious exception of color, would cover a very wide range of contemporary products. Omitting color, many American domestic beers, for example, could fall somewhere between Watney's Cream Stout and Carbine Stout! Nevertheless, the commercial stouts used in our tests are stout indeed (table 5.2). They fall mostly in the range 4.5 to 7.5 percent alcohol by volume (3.5 to 5.9 percent alcohol by weight) with intense black color equivalent to our stouts made with 9 percent roasted material inclusion; some have a pH below 4 and most have a pH below 4.33. Both imperial stouts (Grant's and Samuel Smith's) are high in alcohol (6.30 and 7.37 percent alcohol by volume respectively) but plenty of stouts not called imperial contained as much alcohol, including Dragon Stout (7.59 percent alcohol by volume). Presumably, whatever quality defines "imperialness," it isn't alcohol! Many, but not all, of the stouts show a high real degree of fermentation (RDF). The stouts fall mainly into two categories for this analytical value: 62 percent and above, and below 56 percent. Though we can by no means be sure, high RDF implies ample opportunity for ß-amylase action in mashing and/or addition of fermentable extract as syrup (for example, Old Australian), and a low RDF implies inhibited action of ß-amylase in mashing and/or addition of unfermentable extract as with the lactose in Mackeson.

MIXED GAS DISPENSE

A mixture of nitrogen and carbon dioxide was introduced many years ago by Guinness for draught dispense of their stout. (The term "draft" in the United States originally meant draught dispense, but now can also mean unpasteurized beer, like draft bottled beer). Mixed gas dispense technology has now been adopted by other brewers. The head dispensed onto the beer by use of nitrogen under pressure is akin to the head of foam on beers dispensed through traditional hand pumps (beer engines). These devices tend to squirt the beer into a glass, which causes breakout of the relatively small amount of carbon dioxide present, creating a creamy head supported by air (mostly nitrogen). Draught Guinness in a can (a different product from Guinness Extra) has recently been introduced in which the same surge of gas-liquid separation seen in a pint of Guinness on draught in a pub can now be enjoyed at home. Of course the gas surge is not merely cosmetic: it brings up the famous fine white Guinness foam head and stabilizes it and substantially decarbonates the stout. As a result the stout with its thick creamy head acquires a mellow richness and texture different from and not possible with a beer gassed and dispensed with carbon dioxide alone. Some other brewers have adopted this mode of dispense, not only for their draught stouts, but also for suitable ales. Craft-brewed ales and stouts in the United States would seem natural candidates for this technology, as they would for the traditional hand-pump method of dispense. Similarly, the in-can system (ICS) for causing gas breakout is now used by several British brewers, each with their own design, and its use is not restricted to stouts.

Nitrogen effectively stabilizes the foam of the draught product because when it passes through the small holes in a Guinness tap the stout receives a high shear. This causes the nitrogen and carbon dioxide to break out of solution to form very tiny bubbles of rather even size which are inherently stable. The nitrogen, being rather insoluble in beer, then tends to stay in the bubbles, rather than leaking through the bubble walls to form larger, less stable bubbles or to the atmosphere (which is mostly nitrogen), thereby causing the foam to be stable. To achieve sufficient nitrogenation of the stout in kegs high pressure must be used with the already sufficiently carbonated stout; a device appropriately called a nitrogenizer is used for this purpose. Keg Guinness is

TABLE 5.2

Beer Analyzed	SG	OG (°Plato)	ABW %	RE %	RDF %	AE %	ADF %	ABV %	Kilo-Calories	Color	pH
Dragon Stout	1.01611	17.85	5.91	6.76	64.34	4.11	77.000	7.59	243.20	57.89	4.04
Young's Oatmeal Stout	1.01405	13.10	3.99	5.42	60.29	3.59	72.600	5.11	175.70	54.31	4.29
Samuel Smith's Imperial Stout	1.01411	17.03	5.75	6.19	65.73	3.60	78.900	7.37	230.50	59.13	4.32
Samuel Adams Cream Stout	1.01760	13.07	3.59	6.14	54.72	4.48	65.700	4.62	176.90	51.36	4.49
Mackeson Triple Stout	1.02273	14.71	3.77	7.51	50.95	5.76	60.800	4.88	202.10	60.76	4.25
Samuel Smith's Oatmeal Stout	1.01376	12.44	3.73	5.23	59.53	3.51	71.800	4.78	166.40	55.42	3.89
Sierra Nevada Stout	1.01438	16.52	5.48	6.15	64.82	3.67	77.800	7.03	223.40	58.53	4.32
Granti Imperial Stout	1.01480	15.35	4.91	6.02	62.77	3.78	75.400	6.30	207.20	60.81	4.21
Old Australian Stout	1.01135	16.29	5.71	5.48	68.30	2.90	82.200	7.30	218.70	60.10	4.00
Sapporo Black Beer	1.01213	13.03	4.16	5.01	63.14	3.10	76.200	5.32	173.70	46.99	4.33
Stallion Stout	1.01704	17.04	5.43	6.80	62.28	4.34	74.500	6.99	232.20	60.48	4.45
Anderson Valley Oatmeal Stout	1.02238	15.78	4.28	7.64	53.66	5.67	64.000	5.54	216.80	60.76	4.32
Lost Coast Stout	1.02325	17.21	4.84	8.10	55.23	5.89	65.800	6.26	237.50	61.06	4.26
Guinness Extra Stout	1.00951	13.29	4.55	4.52	67.55	2.44	81.700	5.81	176.00	54.15	4.11
Steelhead Stout	1.02786	15.37	3.52	8.67	45.65	7.03	54.300	4.58	213.80	61.14	4.02
Old #38 Stout	1.01408	13.67	4.24	5.54	61.23	3.59	73.700	5.43	183.50	52.90	4.34
Rogue Shakespeare Stout	1.02084	13.49	3.44	6.89	50.77	5.29	60.800	4.44	184.30	60.35	4.35
Samuel Smith's Taddy Porter	1.00997	11.93	3.91	4.35	64.97	2.55	78.600	4.99	157.70	52.83	3.89
Mendocino Blackhawk Stout	1.01028	14.07	4.82	4.83	67.34	2.63	81.300	6.16	187.10	60.20	4.23
Carbine Stout	1.01084	12.31	3.98	4.61	64.09	2.77	77.500	5.09	163.20	52.88	4.15
Watney's Cream Stout	1.01488	11.53	3.21	5.29	55.66	3.80	67.100	4.12	154.50	58.49	4.03

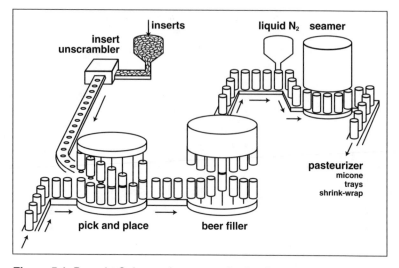

Figure 5.1. Draught Guinness in cans packaging line.

fully nitrogenated on-line to the keg in this way. The dispense gas must then be correctly formulated according to Henry's Law to keep both the carbon dioxide and nitrogen in solution in the stout. This formula usually results in a mixture between 40/60 percent and 30/70 percent carbon dioxide/nitrogen by volume. Draught Guinness for canning is partially nitrogenated by the nitrogenator (up to 0.5 percent volumes by volume [v/v]). To avoid excessive fobbing when the can is filled, the nitrogen level is topped up after filling and before seaming with liquid nitrogen dosed into each can. Simply pouring such nitrogenated stout from a small package generates insufficient shear force to promote adequate gas breakout compared to the classical gas surge in a glass. To imitate the events of draught dispense the can must contain a device that generates a high shear force. The in-can system or ICS (much more interestingly called the draught flow system by Murphy's model of the same product now available in the United States) was therefore developed.

The ICS is a nitrogen-filled plastic chamber with a minute hole placed in the base of a 500-milliliter can. Each can is then filled with 440 milliliters of properly gassed and (to retain gas) very cold stout plus a small dose of liquid nitrogen (figure 5.1). The Guinness patent

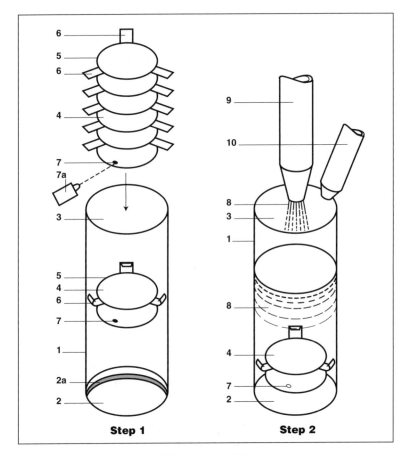

Figure 5.2. Insertion of the ICS and stout filling.

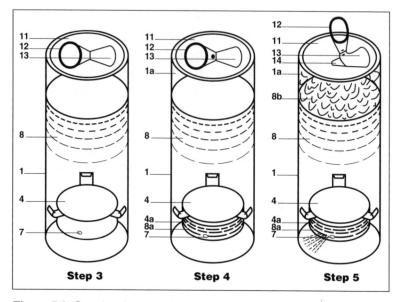

Figure 5.3. Opening the can; shear and gas nucleation.

calls for dissolved nitrogen in the range 1.5 to 3.5 percent volumes by volume (v/v) — achieved in the nitrigenator and by dosing liquid nitrogen into the can just before seaming — and carbon dioxide at 0.8 to 1.8 volumes (1.5 to 3.3 grams per liter). Depending on the market, contemporary nitrogen level might be 3.0 to 5.0 percent alcohol v/v nitrogen and 1.8 to 2.2 grams per liter carbon dioxide. After closing, the can develops over 25 pounds per square inch gauge (psig) pressure. This high pressure, developed especially during pasteurization, forces stout into the interior of the ICS which substantially fills with stout and, over time, the head space pressure in the ICS and the can equilibrate. When the ring-pull is removed the excess pressure in the can is released to atmosphere and the beer-gas mixture in the ICS squirts out of the narrow hole, generating a small but intense stream of beer with sufficient shear to cause gas breakout; these bubbles in turn nucleate other bubbles and the characteristic Guinness surge is underway. The large can permits expansion of the foam head in the can before the stout is poured into a glass. As long as the stout is cold and several seconds are allowed for the foam to develop in the can before pouring, the rewards of this technology for the consumer are great. These events are well illustrated in figures 5.2 and 5.3 taken from the original Guinness patent (no. GB 2,183,592 B).

6

Brewing Stouts at Home

BY ASHTON LEWIS

I frequently hear homebrewers discussing the relative difficulty of brewing various beer styles and have come to the realization that many people feel stout is the easiest style of beer to brew at home. This idea seems to be related to the fact that stouts are quite flavorful and are presumably better able to hide their flaws than, say, light beers, which have flavors that are far too delicate to hide any blemishes. I agree with this argument if the beer's flaw is an odd yeast character or a slight microbiological problem. However, poorly formulated stouts are equally, if not more, unpleasant to the consumer than other ill-conceived beers. In my opinion, stouts should come very close to, but certainly not exceed, the outer limit of roasted malt and hop bitterness characters that are acceptable in a beverage that has historically been quaffed in large volumes over long sessions. This is not an easy task. Few stouts in the world are "just right" for my palate. Many tend to lack enough roasted flavor, hop bitterness, or body while others do not fit my idea of drinkable, and taste like cold, fizzy, very bitter, very acrid espresso. Based upon my own observations, I have concluded that a great stout is a balanced stout and, like any other balanced beer, is not any simpler to make at home than other beer styles. However, if a friend spits your stout on the floor complaining that it tastes like motor oil, you can take the easy out and blame it on the style! Perhaps *this* is why people think that stouts are the easiest of all beer styles to brew at home.

MILLING

The easiest and most practical approach to milling grist for stout brews is to mill all of your grains using the same mill gap. You should adjust your mill so that the pale malt is coarsely milled, yielding a grist containing large pieces of intact husk and broken endosperm with little flour. If you wish to optimize the yield of the various grains used in stout brewing, then adjusting the roller gap for each raw material will be required. As mentioned earlier, roasted barley is milled very finely for Guinness Stout. In my research experience with the pilot brewery at the University of California–Davis, I found that flaked barley should also be finely milled. Commercial brewers accomplish this with special adjunct mills. We use a large coffee mill, and homebrewers may wish to use a blender. Either method is acceptable.

The most important thing to consider when milling is that you obtain an acceptable extract yield from your chosen raw materials without causing lautering problems by milling too finely. Homebrewers should try to keep things simple by milling coarsely and by not worrying too much about extract yield since the loss of extract in a five-gallon batch caused by milling too coarsely will most likely cost less than fifty cents!

Rightfully so, commercial brewers are a bit more concerned with extract yield.

WATER

Like all other beers, water for stout brewing should be potable and have little or no aroma, especially from chlorine. If your town's water is naturally high in carbonates, I would recommend using it. If you are dealing with hard water that is low in carbonates (temporary hardness), however, I would suggest adjusting it or using distilled water and adding salts. All mashes benefit from some calcium since calcium stabilizes alpha-amylase. Therefore, if you are starting with distilled water add 215 milligrams per liter gypsum or 140 milligrams per liter of calcium chloride to obtain 50 parts per million (ppm) of calcium. The next step is to add carbonate to your water. This can be accomplished by using either calcium carbonate or sodium bicarbonate. I prefer sodium bicarbonate since it is soluble in water and low concentrations of sodium add some palate fullness to beer. If you use calcium carbonate it must be dissolved in acidified water — the same way it is dissolved from tea pots with weak acid — or directly added to the mash (which has a low enough pH to bring the carbonate into solution as bicarbonate) to yield the concentrations required for stout brewing. Remember that the goal of all this water adjustment is to obtain a range of 5.2 to 5.4 mash pH. If mash pH is too low, increase carbonate levels in subsequent brews; if too high, decrease carbonate levels.

MASHING

Historically, stouts have been made using the infusion mash. This method has stood the test of time and still works great for stout brewing. A mash temperature of 150 to 154 degrees F (66 to 68 degrees C) and a liquor-to-grist ratio of 2.5:1 to 3:1 should be used for your infusion mash. After one to one and a half hours, raise the temperature to 170 degrees F (77 degrees C) for mash-off and begin running the wort from the mash. After collecting the first runnings, begin sparging with 170 degrees F (77 degrees C) water that has been adjusted like that used for mashing. You should collect enough wort to allow for a one-and-a-half-hour boil. This, of course, depends on your particular system.

Infusion mashing works well for most purposes. However, if you plan on sterile-filtering your stout and are going to use flaked barley in its formulation, infusion mashing may be inadequate. Under these circumstances I would include a ß-glucanase rest at 120 degrees F (49 degrees C) for thirty minutes to reduce the size of ß-glucans found in raw barley. If this step is not included, it is likely that your sterile filter will quickly become blinded by these gummy biopolymers.

WORT BOILING

Boil wort for one to one and a half hours, adding all of the bittering hops one hour before the end of the boil. The boil should be a full-rolling, vigorous boil. If brewing at home, a large pot should be used to reduce the chance of boil-overs. Kettle finings, such as Irish moss, can be added during the last fifteen minutes of the boil. The use of kettle finings, although not necessary for a stout's clarity, have been demonstrated to improve foam stability by removing foam-negative protein fractions from wort. After boiling, cool the wort as rapidly as possible to your desired fermentation temperature and aerate.

FERMENTATION

Stout, like other ales, should be pitched with yeast at a concentration of approximately one million cells per milliliters per °Plato. Based upon numerous cell counts that I have performed using hemocytometers and spectrophotometers, I recommend using about 250 milliliters of fairly thick yeast slurry per five gallons of 12 °Plato wort to achieve twelve million cells per milliliter. If you are using dry yeast, fourteen grams will give about the same cell count, assuming a viability between 80 and 95 percent. These pitching rates should be varied accordingly for worts of strengths different from 12 °Plato or 1.048 kilograms per liter.

I like to carry out my fermentations between 65 and 68 degrees F (18 and 20 degrees C). If you want more estery/fruity flavors, a higher fermentation temperature can be used. Once the yeast has flocculated and fermentation is complete, hold the beer at fermentation temperature for one to two days to reduce diacetyl and then cool to 35 to 40 degrees F (2 to 4 degrees C) and store for one week. After this cold storage period, you can bottle, filter, keg, or whatever you choose to do with your stout.

PACKAGING AND DISPENSE

Stout has, perhaps, more options for packaging and dispense than any other beer style. It can simply be carbonated to "normal" levels (2.2. to 2.6 volumes) and served from keg or bottle. A more exciting and rewarding practice is to carbonate your stout to low levels, between one and two volumes, and dispense it from a hand pump or (the ultimate practice) dispense from a Guinness-style tap using mixed gas. In the latter case, you must equilibrate your stout with a mixture of 60 percent nitrogen and 40 percent carbon dioxide at twenty-five pounds per square inch gauge (psig) or 40 pounds per square inch absolute (psia) at a temperature of 38 degrees F (3 degrees C). Since 40 percent of 40 psia is 16 psia or 1.07 psig, your stout will contain approximately 1.2 volumes of carbon dioxide. Once equilibrated under these conditions, you will want to dispense your stout at the same temperature and pressure with the 60/40 gas blend. If you are interested in the Guinness dispense system and want more details, refer to articles by Carroll[14] and Hedderick.[15] If you are a microbrewer or pubbrewer and want to nitrogenate your stouts, remember that these pressures exceed one bar of pressure. In most states, that means that you must use an ASME vessel rated for at least one and one-half bar of pressure to legally treat your stout. Of course in any brewery it is always *safest* not to exceed a vessel's rated working pressure.

All types of stout can be bottled or kegged and can be conventionally carbonated or carbonated at lower levels and dispensed with hand pumps or Guinness-type taps. In my opinion, however, low-gravity stouts should be put on either hand pumps or Guinness-type taps. If conventionally carbonated, they simply fail to exhibit their truly delicious flavors. Another benefit to lower levels of carbon dioxide is increased drinkability. I suppose this may be dangerous in high-gravity beers, but in low-gravity stouts with less alcohol than a Miller Lite, it's a great benefit!

RECIPE FORMULATION

Although not specific to stout formulation, the following section explains how brews are calculated at the University of California–Davis. This information will allow you to change your formulations as raw material yields change, and to give the homebrewer better control when fine-tuning formulations.

Malt. We use percent of total extract derived from various malts as the basis for malt calculations. For example, 80 percent pale malt means that 80 percent of the wort's extract or soluble solids measured by hydrometer is derived from pale malt. This weight will vary depending upon the desired gravity post-boiling, the desired wort volume, and the extract yield of the particular malt. The use of percent extract becomes somewhat confusing when using special malts. For example, 10 percent roast barley in twenty liters of a 12 °Plato wort may be 450 grams, but be nine hundred grams in a 24 °Plato wort. However, 450 grams per twenty liters will give half the roast barley character of nine hundred grams per twenty liters. Therefore, when using special malts I keep this in mind. Since most brews I make are in the OG 1.044 to 1.056 range, 5 percent of special malt "A" will lend a predictable flavor. However, when making low- or high-gravity brews I will adjust up or down with the wort gravity. Although this all seems somewhat awkward, with a little practice this method becomes quite easy.

Step 1

Calculate Weight of Extract

Weight of extract = (desired volume) (desired SG†) (desired °P††)

Step 2

Calculate Weight of Extract

$$\text{Weight of malt} = \frac{(\text{weight of extract}) \ (\text{percent of total extract})}{(\text{extract yield of particular malt } ††)}$$

† See table 6.1 for conversion between SG and °Plato.
†† See table 6.2 for extract yields of various malts.

Example

Suppose you want to produce a wort with the following properties:
Volume after boiling = 20 L
Original gravity = 1.039 kg wort/L wort
°Plato = 9.75° or 0.0975 kg extract/kg wort
Percent pale malt = 70% with 68% yield
Percent flaked barley = 20% with 75% yield
Percent roasted barley = 10% with 55% yield

Step 1

$$\text{Wt. of extract} = \frac{(20 \text{ L \sout{wort}}) (1.039 \text{ \sout{kg wort}}) (0.0975 \text{ kg extract})}{(\text{L \sout{wort}}) (\text{\sout{kg wort}})}$$

$$= 2.026 \text{ kg extract}$$

Step 2

$$\text{Wt. of pale} = (2.026 \text{ \sout{kg total extract}}) \frac{\left(\dfrac{0.70 \text{ \sout{kg extract from pale}}}{\text{\sout{kg total extract}}} \right)}{\left(\dfrac{0.68 \text{ \sout{kg extract from pale}}}{\text{kg pale}} \right)} = 2.086 \text{ kg pale}$$

$$\text{Wt. of flaked barley} = \frac{(2.026)(0.20)}{(0.75)} = 540 \text{ grams flaked}$$

$$\text{Wt. of roasted barley} = \frac{(2.026)(0.1)}{(0.55)} = 370 \text{ grams roast}$$

TABLE 6.1

Conversion Between Specific Gravity and °Plato

Specific Gravity	°Plato	Specific Gravity	°Plato
1.004	1.0	1.044	11.0
1.008	2.0	1.048	12.0
1.012	3.0	1.053	13.0
1.016	4.0	1.057	14.0
1.020	5.0	1.061	15.0
1.024	6.0	1.065	16.0
1.028	7.0	1.070	17.0
1.032	8.0	1.074	18.0
1.036	9.0	1.079	19.0
1.040	10.0	1.083	20.0

Hops. We use a straightforward method to calculate hopping rates. The basis for the calculation is International Bittering Units (IBU). There are many other hop calculations used by brewers to calculate such things as aroma, but we find this method to be fairly accurate and reproducible for calculating bitterness.

$$\text{Wt. of hops (grams)} = \frac{\text{(wort volume after boil) (desired IBU)}}{\text{(\% alpha of hop) (\% utilization) (1,000)}}$$

For example, suppose you want to produce twenty liters of wort with 37 IBU using Kent Goldings hops with 5.5 percent alpha acid. Figure on about 30 percent utilization if these hops are boiled for sixty to ninety minutes. Since I have measured this on the University of California–Davis system, I know that 30 percent utilization is typical for normal gravity worts. Most homebrew

TABLE 6.2

Extract Yields of Selected Raw Materials

Raw Material	Percent Yield	Raw Material	Percent Yield
Pale Malt	70%	Roasted Malt	55%
Wheat Malt	80%	Roasted Barley	55%
Munich Malt	70%	Flaked Barley	75%
Crystal Malt	60%	Rice Syrup	75%
Amber/Brown Malt	60%	Malt Syrup	75%
Chocolate Malt	55%	Dry Malt Extract	95%

systems will have about 25 percent utilization. I use 5 percent as my utilization for hops added ten to fifteen minutes before the end of boiling, and for moderate additions (less than two ounces) made within the last five minutes I assume no bitterness added. If you do not know your hop utilization, there have been several articles in *Zymurgy®*, *The New Brewer*, *MBAA TQ*, among others, and a new book, *Using Hops*, by Mark Garetz, that explore this topic in depth.

$$\text{Wt. of hops (g)} = \frac{(20 \text{ L wort})\left(37 \frac{\text{mg iso alpha acids}}{\text{L wort}}\right)}{\left(\frac{0.055 \text{ g alpha}}{\text{g hops}}\right)\left(\frac{0.30 \text{ g iso alpha}}{\text{g alpha}}\right)\left(\frac{1{,}000 \text{ mg}}{\text{g}}\right)} = 45 \text{ g or } \sim 1.5 \text{ oz}$$

This brief description of brewing procedures and recipe formulation is intended to serve as a general overview of the stout brewing process. I know there are some readers grinding their teeth wishing they could debate some minor point of this chapter with me.

That's okay because I am a brewer and, like most other brewers, am opinionated. So if you have different ideas please use them to increase the diversity of stouts in the beer kingdom!

STOUT RECIPES

The following recipes include all of the information needed to calculate the amount of each ingredient required. I strongly suggest that you get into the habit of calculating your own recipes to reflect your unique system. However, since this book is supposed to make life a little easier, I have calculated these recipes for *my* system. If you decide to use my recipes as is, you will definitely be in the ballpark! You will notice that I use kilograms, grams, and liters in these recipes. If you want to convert these to English units you can multiply kilograms by 2.2046 to get pounds, divide grams by 28.3495 to convert to ounces, and multiply liters by 0.2641 to switch to gallons.

All of these stout recipes, except for the Irish Draught Stout, can be used by extract brewers by substituting malt syrup or dry malt extract for pale malt. If using extracts, multiply the weight of pale malt by 0.93 to determine the weight of malt syrup to use or multiply by 0.74 to determine the weight of dry malt extract. When I brew with extracts, I put my milled special malts in a large bag fashioned from cheese cloth and steep them in ten liters of 170 degree F (97 degree C) brew water for thirty minutes. I then lift the bag out and gently pour about five liters of sparge water over the bag. Once this process is complete I add my extract, increase the total wort volume to twenty-four liters, and carry out the boil. My system evaporates five liters of water per hour, so after a one-hour boil this procedure gives me nineteen liters, or right at five gallons, of wort.

WEST COAST STOUT

		5 Gallons (Grain)	1 Barrel (Grain)
Extract Source			
Pale Malt	83%	3.2 kg	19.84 kg
Roasted Malt	12%	600 g	3.72 kg
Dark Crystal	5%	180 g	1.12 kg
Bittering Hops			
Cluster (6% alpha)	50 IBU	53 g	330 g
Aroma Hops			
Cascade	Steep	56 g	350 g
Specifics			
Mash water volume	—	12 liters	74 liters
Liquor:Grist Ratio	3:1		
Mash Temperature	154°F (68°C)		
Original Gravity	1.054 (13.5°P)		
Priming sugar	8.3 g sugar/L beer		
Carbonation	2.6 volumes		
Packaging	bottle or keg		
Maturation Time	2 to 4 weeks		

137

IRISH DRAUGHT STOUT

		5 Gallons (Grain)	1 Barrel (Grain)
Extract Source			
Pale Malt	70%	1.9 kg	11.78 kg
Roasted Barley	10%	340 g	2.1 kg
Flaked Barley	20%	500 g	3.1 kg
Bittering Hops			
East Kent Golding			
(5.5% alpha)	37 IBU	42 g	260 g
Specifics			
Mash water volume	—	8 liters	50 liters
Liquor:Grist Ratio	3:1		
Mash Temperature	152°F (67°C)		
Original Gravity	1.038 (9.5°P)		
Priming sugar	2.8 g sugar/L beer		
Carbonation	1.2 volumes		
Packaging	keg		
Dispense	mixed gas or pump		
Maturation Time	2 to 4 weeks		

DRY STOUT (Bottled)

		5 Gallons (Grain)	1 Barrel (Grain)
Extract Source			
Pale Malt	72%	2.9 kg	18 kg
Roasted Barley	8%	410 g	2.5 kg
Rice Syrup	20%	700 g	4.3 kg
Bittering Hops			
East Kent Golding			
(5.5% alpha)	55 IBU	63 g	390 g
Specifics			
Mash water volume	—	12 liters	74 liters
Liquor:Grist Ratio	3:1		
Mash Temperature	152°F (67°C)		
Original Gravity	1.056 (14°P)		
Priming sugar	7.5 g sugar/L beer		
Carbonation	2.4 volumes		
Packaging	bottle		
Maturation Time	2 to 4 weeks		

SWEET STOUT

		5 Gallons (Grain)	1 Barrel (Grain)
Extract Source			
Pale Malt	85%	2.9 kg	18 kg
Roasted Malt	7%	300 g	1.9 kg
Dark Crystal	5%	160 g	900 g
Chocolate Malt	3%	130 g	800 g
Bittering Hops			
East Kent Golding			
(5.5% alpha)	25 IBU	29 g	180 g
Specifics			
Mash water volume	—	10 liters	62 liters
Liquor:Grist Ratio	3:1		
Mash Temperature	154°F (68°C)		
Original Gravity	1.048 (12°P)		
Lactose (add when bottling)	53 g/L		
Priming sugar	7.5 g sugar/L beer		
Carbonation	2.4 volumes		
Packaging	bottle		
Maturation Time	4 to 6 weeks		

CARIBBEAN STOUT

		5 Gallons (Grain)	1 Barrel (Grain)
Extract Source			
Pale Malt	73.75%	3.7 kg	23 kg
Roasted Barley	4%	260 g	1.6 kg
Dark Crystal	5%	240 g	1.5 kg
Chocolate Malt	2.25%	145 g	900 g
Rice Syrup	15%	665 g	4.1 kg
Bittering Hops			
East Kent Golding			
(5.5% alpha)	35 IBU	40 g	250 g
Specifics			
Mash water volume	—	15 liters	93 liters
Liquor:Grist Ratio	3:1		
Mash Temperature	156°F (69°C)		
Original Gravity	1.070 (17.5°P)		
Priming sugar	6 g sugar/L beer		
Carbonation	2.0 volumes		
Packaging	bottle		
Maturation Time	4 to 12 weeks		

IMPERIAL STOUT

		5 Gallons (Grain)	1 Barrel (Grain)
Extract Source			
Pale Malt	88%	5.7 kg	35 kg
Roasted Barley	3.5%	290 g	1.8 kg
Dark Crystal	3%	210 g	1.3 kg
Chocolate Malt	2.5%	210 g	1.3 kg
Brown Malt	3%	180 g	1.1 kg
Bittering Hops			
East Kent Golding			
(5.5% alpha)	50 IBU	69 g	430 g
Aroma Hops			
East Kent Golding	Steep	56 g	350 g
Specifics			
Mash water volume	—	20 liters	124 liters
Liquor:Grist Ratio	3:1		
Mash Temperature	156°F (69°C)		
Original Gravity	1.088 (22°P)		
Priming sugar	8 g sugar/L beer		
Carbonation	2.5 volumes		
Packaging	bottle		
Maturation Time	6 to 60 months		

Appendix:

Commercial
Stout Breweries

Guinness, St. James's Gate, Dublin;
Smithwick (Guinness), Kilkenny;
Cherry's (Guinness), Waterford;
Harp (Guinness), Dundalk;
Macardle Moore (Guinness),
Dundalk

"Guinness Extra Stout": OG 1.040,
ABV 4.3%. Massive hop presence
with pronounced roast barley notes.
Ripe bittersweet balance with tart
fruit and great length of hops, fruit,
coffee, and chocolate notes. A world classic, jet black beer of enormous complexity and character.

James A. Murphy's Ltd., Cork, Ireland
"Murphy's Irish Stout": Distinctively toasty tasting, malty, and very dry.

Beamish and Crawford, Cork, Ireland
"Beamish Genuine Stout": OG 1.039, ABV 4.2%. Creamy, chocolatey, and least dry of the Irish stouts.

Photographs courtesy of Merchant Du Vin.

ENGLAND, SCOTLAND, AND WALES

Northeast England

Butterknowle Brewery, Lynesack, Butterknowle, Bishop Auckland, County Durham
"Festival Stout": OG 1.038, ABV 3.6%. Malty, biscuity aroma with light hop notes. Tasty dark beer with chewy grain and hops character.

North Yorkshire Brewing Co., Middlesborough, Cleveland
"Erimus Dark Stout": OG 1.046. Warm aromas of roasted barley and hops. Mellow in the mouth with creamy nut and light fruit. Smooth drinking with a soft creamy head.

Yorkshire:
Linfit Brewery, Linthwaite, Huddersfield
"English Guineas Stout": OG 1.050, ABV 5%. Promising aromas of hops and roast barley, rich nut and hop prickle on the tongue with a dry chocolatey finish. Tasty dark stout with a gravity closer to the original eighteenth-century style than most modern commercial stouts.

John Smith's Tadcaster Brewery, Tadcaster, North Yorkshire (Subsidiary of Courage/Foster's)
"Imperial Russian Stout" (bottle conditioned): OG 1.104, ABV 10%. This big stout is rumored to be hopped at a rate of 24 lbs. per barrel. Stunningly dry, bitter, black, chocolate on tongue with deep intense finish. Not for the faint hearted!

Samuel Smith Ole Brewery, Tadcaster, North Yorkshire
"Oatmeal Stout": OG 1.050, 5.0%.
"Imperial Russian Stout": OG 1.072, ABV 7.0%. Powerful and fruity stout.

Central England

Burton Bridge Brewery, Burton upon Trent, Staffordshire
"Top Dog Stout": OG 1.050, ABV 5%. Rich roast barley and biscuits aroma. Bitter barley and hops in mouth, deep dry finish with bitter chocolate, hops and rich fruit notes. This superb stout is brewed only in the winter.

Hoskins & Oldfield, North Mills, Frog Island, Leicester
"Tom Kelley's Stout": OG 1.043. Bitter and chocolate and malt aromas with good hop notes. Strong dark malt in mouth, long finish with dark chocolate and hop notes. A fine tasting bitter stout.

Jolly Roger Brewery, Lowesmoore, Worcester
"Goodness Stout": OG 1.042, ABV 4.2%. Tempting chocolate and coffee aroma with good hop edge. Intensely bitter in the mouth, long dry finish with assertive hop character and black chocolate notes.

Premier Ales Ltd., Stourbridge, West Midlands
"Black Knight Stout": OG 1.050, ABV 5%. Nutty aromas of roasted grain and hop, smooth malt and hop balance with dry finish and nut and fruit notes. A fine jet black stout, silkily drinkable.

Eastern England

Banks and Taylor Brewing Ltd., Shefford, Bedfordshire
"Edwin Taylor's Extra Stout": OG 1.042, ABV 4.2%. Pungent aromas of roasted grain, bitter chocolate and a hop resin. Ripe malt with strong roast notes and deep, balanced finished. A superb stout with exceptional hoppiness and bitter malt character.

Maudons Brewery, Sudbury, Suffolk
"Black Adder": OG 1.055, ABV 5.2%. Roast and nut aromas with a fine fruity balance of hop and dark malt in the mouth, intensely long dry finish with coffee and nut notes. Grainy, chewy, memorably tasty strong stout.

The Reepham Brewery, Reepham, Norfolk
"Smugglers Stout": OG 1.074, ABV 4.8%. Burnt toast, rich hop and malt aromas. Deep bitter flavors of charred malt, long intensely dry finish and coffee notes. A red/black stout with deep complex flavors.

London

Park Royal Brewery (Guinness) London
"Draught Stout": Packaged using Guinness's unique in-can system.

Young's & Co., Wandsworth (near London)
"Oatmeal Stout": Light, but very smooth with a touch of oily dryness.

West Country

Cotleigh Brewery, Wilveliscombe, Somerset
"Old Buzzard Stout": OG 1.048, ABV 4.8%. Roast chestnut and coffee aromas, rich chewy malt in the mouth, and deep finish with hops and hints of black chocolate.

Northwest England

Whitbread's Mackeson Brewing Company, Samlesbury, Lancashire
"Mackeson Stout": As one of the original milk stouts this heavy, rich stout tastes likes sweetened espresso.

AUSTRIA

Schloss Brew Pub and Winery, Nussdorf
"Sir Henry's Stout": ABV 6%.

NORWAY

Akershus Brewery
"Irish Stout"

Ceres Brewery, Aarhus
"Stout"

HOLLAND

Heineken Breweries Ltd., Amsterdam
"Van Vollenhovens Stout," OG 1.065, ABV

CANADA

Brewsters, Calgary, British Columbia
"Stout"

Conners Brewery, St. Catherine, Ontario
"Stout"

McAuslan, Montreal, Quebec
"Oatmeal Stout, Biere Noire"

Niagra Falls Brewing, Niagra, Ontario
"Brocks Extra Stout"

Okanagan Spring, Vernon, British Columbia
"Saint Patrick's Stout"

Spinakers, Victoria, British Columbia
"Empress Stout"

Swan's, Victoria, British Columbia
"Oatmeal Stout"

Wellington County, Guelph, Ontario
"Imperial Stout," ABV 8.0%

ASIA

Kirin Breweries, Tokyo, Japan
"Kirin Stout," ABV 8.0%

Stout

Asahi Breweries Ltd., Tokyo, Japan
"Stout"

Asia-Pacific Breweries, China
"ABC Extra Stout," OG 1.073, ABV 8.1%

SRI LANKA

McCallum Breweries, Sri Lanka
"Sando Stout," OG 1.060

AUSTRALIA

Cascade Breweries, Hobart, Tasmania
"Stout"

Castlemaine Perkins Ltd., Brisbane, Queensland
"Carbine Stout"

Coopers, Adelaide
"Stout," ABV 6.8%

Foster's, Melbourne, Victoria
"Abbot's Double Stout"

Geebung Polo Club, Melbourne, Victoria
"Razorback Stout"

Od Goulburn, Sydney
"Stout"

Sail and Anchor, Fremantle, Western Australia
"Brass Monkey Stout"

Shakespeare, Auckland
"Stout"

Southern Australia Brewing, Adelaide
"Stout," ABV 7.6%

Tooth's, Sydney (Subsidiary of Foster's)
"Sheaf Stout," ABV 5.7%

SOUTH AFRICA

South African Breweries, Johannesburg
"Castle Milk Stout"

UNITED STATES

Brooklyn Brewery, Brooklyn, New York
"Brooklyn Black Chocolate Stout"

Coyote Springs Brewing Co. & Cafe, Phoenix, Arizona
"Bolshevik's Delight," "Oatmeal Stout," "Old Quaker"

Goose Island Brewing Co., Chicago, Illinois
"Irish Stout," "Honest Stout," "Sweet Stout," "Russian Imperial Stout"

Hales Ales, Kirkland, Washington
"Moss Bay Stout"

Hart Brewing Co./Pyramid Ales, Seattle, Washington
"Hart Espresso Stout," "Sphinx Stout"

Kalamazoo Brewing Co. Inc., Kalamazoo, Michigan
"Bell's Cherry Stout," "Bell's Kalamazoo Stout"

Marin Brewing Company, Larkspur, California
"San Quentin's Breakout Stout"

Miller Brewing Company, Milwaukee, Wisconsin
"Miller Reserve Velvet Stout"

Oasis Brewery, Boulder, Colorado
"Zoser Stout"

Old Dominion Brewing Co., Ashburn, Virginia
"Dominion Stout"

Pike Place Brewery, Seattle, Washington
"XXXXX Stout"

Port City Brewery, Mobile, Alabama
"Admiral Semmes' Stout"

Sierra Nevada Brewing Co., Chico, California
"Sierra Nevada Stout"

Note: This is only a partial listing of the numerous brewers of stout.

Glossary

adjunct. Any unmalted grain or other fermentable ingredient added to the mash.

aeration. The action of introducing air to the wort at various stages of the brewing process.

airlock. *See* fermentation lock.

airspace. *See* ullage.

alcohol by volume (v/v). The percentage of volume of alcohol per volume of beer. To calculate the approximate volumetric alcohol content, subtract the terminal gravity from the original gravity and divide the result by 75. For example: $1.050 - 1.012 = 0.038 / 0.0075 = 5\%$ v/v.

alcohol by weight (w/v). The percentage weight of alcohol per volume of beer. For example: 3.2% alcohol by weight = 3.2 grams of alcohol per 100 centiliters of beer. Alcohol by weight can be converted to alcohol by volume by multiplying by 0.795.

aldehyde. A contraction of alcohol dehydrogenate. These compounds are characterized as oxidized alcohols, with a terminal CHO group.

ale. 1. Historically, an unhopped malt beverage; 2. Now a generic term for hopped beers produced by top fermentation, as opposed to lagers, which are produced by bottom fermentation.

all-extract beer. A beer made with only malt extract as opposed to one made from barley, or a combination of malt extract and barley.

all-grain beer. A beer made with only malted barley as opposed to one made from malt extract, or from malt extract and malted barley.

all-malt beer. A beer made with only barley malt with no adjuncts or refined sugars.

alpha acid. A soft resin in hop cones. When boiled, alpha acids are converted to iso-alpha-acids, which account for 60 percent of a beer's bitterness.

alpha-acid unit (AAU). A measurement of the potential bitterness of hops, expressed by their percentage of alpha acid. Low = 2 to 4%; medium = 5 to 7%; high = 8 to 12%.

alt. The german word for old. This is an old-fashioned, top-fermenting style of beer that undergoes a cold lagering for maturation.

amino acids. The building blocks of proteins. Essential components of wort, required for adequate yeast growth.

attenuation. The reduction in the wort's specific gravity caused by the transformation of sugars into alcohol and carbon-dioxide gas.

Balling. A saccharometer invented by Carl Joseph Napoleon Balling in 1843. It is calibrated for 63.5 degrees F (17.5 degrees C), and graduated in grams per hundred, giving a direct reading of the percentage of extract by weight per 100 grams solution. For example: 10 °B = 10 grams of sugar per 100 grams of wort.

blow-by (blow-off). A single-stage homebrewing fermentation method in which a plastic tube is fitted into the mouth of a carboy, with the other end submerged in a pail of sterile water. Unwanted residues and carbon dioxide are expelled through the tube, while air is prevented from coming into contact with the fermenting beer, thus avoiding contamination.

carbonation. The process of introducing carbon-dioxide gas into a liquid by: 1. injecting the finished beer with carbon dioxide; 2. adding young fermenting beer to finished beer for a renewed fermentation (kraeusening); 3. priming (adding sugar) to fermented wort prior to bottling, creating a secondary fermentation in the bottle; 4. finishing fermentation under pressure.

carboy. A large glass, plastic, or earthenware bottle.

chill haze. Haziness caused by protein and tannin during the secondary fermentation.

dimethyl sulfide (DMS). An important sulfur-carrying compound originating in malt. Adds a crisp, "lager-like" character at low levels and corn or cabbage flavors at high levels.

dry hopping. The addition of hops to the primary fermenter, the secondary fermenter, or to casked beer to add aroma and hop character to the finished beer without adding significant bitterness.

dry malt. Malt extract in powdered form.

EBC (European Brewery Convention). *See* SRM.

ester. A class of organic compounds created from the reaction of an alcohol and an organic acid. These tend to have fruity aromas and are detectable at low concentrations.

extract. The amount of dissolved materials in the wort after mashing and lautering malted barley and/or malt adjuncts such as corn and rice.

fermentation lock. A one-way valve, which allows carbon-dioxide gas to escape from the fermenter while excluding contaminants.

final specific gravity. The specific gravity of a beer when fermentation is complete.

fining. The process of adding clarifying agents to beer during secondary fermentation to precipitate suspended matter.

flocculation. The behavior of yeast cells joining into masses and settling out toward the end of fermentation.

homebrewers bittering units (HBU). A formula invented by the American Homebrewers Association to measure bitterness of beer. Example: 1.5 ounces of hops at 10 percent alpha acid for five gallons: 1.5 x 10 = 15 HBU per five gallons.

hop pellets. Finely powdered hop cones compressed into tablets. Hop pellets are 20 to 30 percent more bitter by weight than the same variety in loose form.

hydrometer. A glass instrument used to measure the specific gravity of liquids as compared to water, consisting of a graduated stem resting on a weighed float.

International Bitterness Unit (IBU). This is an empirical quantity originally designed to measure the concentration of iso-alpha-acids in milligrams per liter (parts per million). Most procedures will also measure a small amount of uncharacter-ized soft resins so IBUs are generally 5 to 10% higher than iso-alpha acid concentrations.

isinglass. A gelatinous substance made from the swim bladder of certain fish and added to beer as a fining agent.

kraeusen. (n.) The rocky head of foam which appears on the surface of the wort during fermentation. (v.) To add ferment-ing wort to fermented beer to induce carbonation through a secondary fermentation.

lager. (n.) A generic term for any bottom-fermented beer. Lager brewing is now the predominant brewing method worldwide except in Britain where top-fermented ales domi-nate. (v.) To store beer at near-zero temperatures in order to precipitate yeast cells and proteins and improve taste.

lauter tun. A vessel in which the mash settles and the grains are removed from the sweet wort through a straining process. It has a false, slotted bottom and spigot.

liquefaction. The process by which alpha-amylase enzymes degrade soluble starch into dextrin.

malt. Barley that has been steeped in water, germinated, then dried in kilns. This process converts insoluble starches to solu-ble substances and sugars.

malt extract. A thick syrup or dry powder prepared from malt.

mashing. Mixing ground malt with water to extract the fer-mentables, degrade haze-forming proteins and convert grain starches to fermentable sugars and nonfermentable carbohydrates.

modification. 1. The physical and chemical changes in barley as a result of malting. 2. The degree to which these changes have occurred, as determined by the growth of the acrospire.

original gravity. The specific gravity of wort previous to fermentation. A measure of the total amount of dissolved solids in wort.

pH. A measure of acidity or alkalinity of a solution, usually on a scale of one to fourteen, where seven is neutral.

Plato. A saccharometer that expresses specific gravity as extract weight in a one-hundred-gram solution at 68 degrees F (20 degrees C). A revised, more accurate version of Balling, developed by Dr. Plato.

polyphenol. Complexes of phenolic compounds involved in chill haze formation and oxidative staling.

primary fermentation. The first stage of fermentation, during which most fermentable sugars are converted to ethyl alcohol and carbon dioxide.

priming sugar. A small amount of corn, malt, or cane sugar added to bulk beer prior to racking or at bottling, to induce a new fermentation and create carbonation.

racking. The process of transferring beer from one container to another, especially into the final package (bottles, kegs, etc.).

saccharification. The naturally occurring process in which malt starch is converted into fermentable sugars, primarily maltose.

saccharometer. An instrument that determines the sugar concentration of a solution by measuring the specific gravity.

secondary fermentation. 1. The second, slower stage of fermentation, which, depending on the type of beer, lasts from a few weeks to many months. 2. A fermentation occurring in bottles or casks and initiated by priming or by adding yeast.

sparging. Spraying the spent grains in the mash with hot water to retrieve the remaining malt sugar.

specific gravity. A measure of a substance's density as compared to that of water, which is given the value of 1.000 at 39.2 degrees F (4 degrees C). Specific gravity has no accompanying units, because it is expressed as a ratio.

SRM (Standard Reference Method) and EBC (European Brewery Convention). Two different analytical methods of describing color developed by comparing color samples. Degrees SRM, approximately equivalent to degrees Lovibond, are used by the ASBC (American Society of Brewing Chemists) while degrees EBC are European units. The following equations show approximate conversions:

$$(°EBC) = 2.65 \times (°Lovibond) - 1.2$$
$$(°Lovibond) = 0.377 \times (°EBC) + 0.45$$

starter. A batch of fermenting yeast, added to the wort to initiate fermentation.

strike temperature. The initial temperature of the water when the malted barley is added to it to create the mash.

tannin. *See* polyphenol.

trub. Suspended particles resulting from the precipitation of proteins, hop oils, and tannins during boiling and cooling stages of brewing.

ullage. The empty space between a liquid and the top of its container. Also called airspace or headspace.

v/v. *See* alcohol by volume.

w/v. *See* alcohol by weight.

water hardness. The degree of dissolved minerals in water.

wort. The mixture that results from mashing the malt and boiling the hops, before it is fermented into beer.

Bibliography

LISTED BY NUMBER

1.   N. B. Redman, "A History of Porter," *The Brewer*, vol. 79 (1993): 255–58.

2.   H. S. Corran, "Source Materials for the History of Brewing," *The Brewer* (October 1974): 583–41.

3.   H. S. Corran, "A History of Brewing," chapter 8 in *The Origin of Porter* (David and Charles Publishers Newton Abbot, 1975).

4.   Various publications of the Guinness Brewery and Guinness Worldwide.

5.   Michael Jackson, *Michael Jackson's Beer Companion* (Philadelphia: Running Press, 1993).

6.   Anton Piendl, *Brauindustrie*, no. 4 (1982): 225–31.

7. National Brewers Academy, *Practical Points for Brewers* (New York: National Brewers Academy, 1993).

8. Robert Wahl and Max Henius, *American Handy-book of Malting and Brewing*, vol. 11 (Chicago: Wahl-Henius Institute, 1908).

9. Roger Bergen, "A Stout Companion," *Brewing Techniques*, vol. 1 (1993): 18–21.

10. *Guinness Stout: A Simple Guide*, a promotional piece published by the Guinness Brewery (August 1992). Various promotional pieces from the company used as a source of information as well.

11. H. Lloyd Hind, *Brewing Science and Practice*, vol. 1 (London: Chapman Hall, 1950): 434–35.

12. Hind, *Brewing Science and Practice*, vol. 1, 254.

13. Institute of Brewing, *Institute of Brewing Blue Book* (London: Institute of Brewing).

14. T.C.N. Carroll, "The Effect of Dissolved Nitrogen Gas on Beer Foam and Palate," *Technical Quarterly of the Master Brewers Association of the Americas*, vol. 3 (1979): 16.

15. J. B. Hedderick, "The Use of Nitrogen for Beer Dispense," *The Brewer* (March 1984).

16. Andy Bielenburg, *Cork's Industrial Revolution, 1780–1880, Development and Decline* (Cork, Ireland: Cork University Press, 1991).

17. Bill Yenne, *Beers of the World* (Greenwich: Brompton Books, 1994).

18. Cormac O'Grada, *Ireland: A New Economic History, 1780–1939* (Oxford: Clarendon Press).

19. Raymond Crotty, *Ireland in Crisis: A Study in Capitalistic Colonial Underdevelopment* (Dingle County, Kerry, Ireland: Brandon Book Publishers): 50

20. A. G. Stark, *The South of Ireland in 1850* (Dublin: Dublin Press, 1850).

21. Beamish and Crawford's to Murphy, 24 March 1901. Cork Archives Institute, Beamish and Crawford's letterbook 1894–1902, Beamish and Crawford's Collection.

22. Michael Jackson, *The New World Guide to Beer* (Philadelphia: Courage Books, 1988).

LISTED BY AUTHOR

Beamish and Crawford. Letter to James A. Murphy's Ltd. on March 24, 1901. Beamish and Crawford's letterbook 1894–1902. Beamish and Crawford's Collection. (21)

Bergen, Roger. "A Stout Companion." *Brewing Techniques* 1 (1993): 18–21. (9)

Bielenburg, Andy. *Cork's Industrial Revolution, 1780–1880, Development and Decline.* Cork, Ireland: Cork University Press, 1991. (16)

Carroll, T.C.N. "The Effect of Dissolved Nitrogen Gas on Beer Foam and Palate." *Technical Quarterly of the Master Brewers Association of the Americas* 3 (1993): 16. (14)

Corran, H. S. "Source Materials for the History of Brewing." *The Brewer* (October 1974): 583–41. (2)

———. "A History of Brewing." In *The Origin of Porter.* Devon, England: David and Charles Publishers, Newton Abbot, 1975. (3)

Crotty, Raymond. *Ireland in Crisis: A Study in Capitalistic Colonial Underdevelopment.* Dingle County, Kerry, Ireland: Brandon Book Publishers. (19)

Guinness Brewery and Guinness Worldwide. References made to their various publications. (4)

———. *Guinness Stout: A Simple Guide.* Ireland: Guinness Brewery, 1992. (10)

Hedderick, J. B. "The Use of Nitrogen for Beer Dispense." *The Brewer* (March 1984). (15)

Hind, H. Lloyd. *Brewing Science and Practice.* Vol. 1. London: Chapman Hall, 1950. (11 and 12)

Institute of Brewing. *Institute of Brewing Blue Book.* London: Institute of Brewing. (13)

Jackson, Michael. *Michael Jackson's Beer Companion.* Philadelphia: Running Press, 1993. (5)

———. *The New World Guide to Beer*. Philadelphia: Courage Books, 1988. (22)

National Brewers Academy. *Practical Points for Brewers*. New York: National Brewers Academy, 1993. (7)

O'Grada, Cormac. *Ireland: A New Economic History, 1780–1939*. Oxford: Clarendon Press. (18)

Piendl, Anton. *Brauindustrie*, no. 4 (1982): 225–31. (6)

Redman, N. B. "A History of Porter." *The Brewer* 79 (1993): 255–58. (1)

Stark, A. G. *The South of Ireland in 1850*. Dublin: Dublin Press, 1850. (20)

Wahl, Robert, and Max Henius. *American Handy-book of Malting and Brewing*. Vol. 11. Chicago: Wahl-Henius Institute, 1908. (8)

Yenne, Bill. *Beers of the World*. Greenwich: Brompton Books, 1994. (17)

Index

ABC Extra Stout, data on, 108-110
Acetaldehyde, 59, 71
  removing, 61
Acetic aroma/taste, 71, 75
ADF. *See* Apparent degree of
  fermentation
AHA list, 85
Akershus Brewery, 147
Aldehydic character, 71, 72, 73, 75
Ales
  brewing, 57
  English/German type, 30 (table)
Alkalinity, 42, 118
  concern about, 43-44
Allen, Aylmer, 17
Allen, Edward, 17
*American Handy-book of Brewing and
  Malting* (Wahl and Henius), 32
Analytical profiles, 86, 118
Anchor Brewery, Russian Stout by, 23
Anchor Porter, PC for, 75
Angel and White Horse (Tadcaster),
  photo of, 29
Apparent degree of fermentation
  (ADF), 118
Arnotts Brewery, 20

Aroma
  calculating, 134
  characters, 82
  terms for, 68 (table), 71
  volatiles, 84
Asahi Breweries Ltd., 148
ASBC flavor wheel, 85
Asia-Pacific Breweries, 148
  stout by, 108-110
Asia, stout breweries in, 147-148
ASME vessels, 131
Astringency, 69, 71, 72, 73, 74, 75
Australia, stout breweries in, 148
Austria, stout breweries in, 146

Bandon Brewing Company, 19
Banks and Taylor Brewing Ltd.,
  25 (map), 145
Banks Breweries Ltd., stout by, 92-94
Barley, 49
  cultivating, 15
  roasting, 7-8, 48
  steaming, 50
  See also Flaked barley
Barley roaster, schematic of, 48 (figure)
Barrett, Richard, 17

BOOKS for Brewers and Beer Lovers

Order Now ... Your Brew Will Thank You!

These books offered by Brewers Publications are some of the most sought after reference tools for homebrewers and professional brewers alike. Filled with tips, techniques, recipes and history, these books will help you expand your brewing horizons. Let the world's foremost brewers help you as you brew. Whatever your brewing level or interest, Brewers Publications has the information necessary for you to brew the best beer in the world — your beer.

- -

Please send me more free information on the following: (check all that apply)

◇ Merchandise and Book Catalog   ◇ Institute for Brewing Studies
◇ American Homebrewers Association® ◇ Great American Beer Festival®

Ship to:

Name

Address

City   State/Province

Zip/Postal Code   Country

Daytime Phone (   )

Please use the following in conjunction with an order form when ordering books from Brewers Publications.

Payment Method

◇ Check or Money Order Enclosed (Payable to the Association of Brewers)
◇ Visa   ◇ MasterCard

Card Number —   —   —   Expiration Date

Name on Card   Signature

Brewers Publications, PO Box 1510, Boulder, CO 80306-1510, U.S.A.; (303) 546-6514; FAX (303) 447-2825

STT

BREWERS PUBLICATIONS ORDER FORM
GENERAL BEER AND BREWING INFORMATION

QTY.	TITLE	STOCK #	PRICE	EXT. PRICE
_____	The Art of Cidermaking................................	468	9.95	_____
_____	Brewing Mead...	461	11.95	_____
_____	Dictionary of Beer and Brewing	462	19.95	_____
_____	Evaluating Beer	465	19.95	_____
_____	Great American Beer Cookbook.....................	466	24.95	_____
_____	New Brewing Lager Beer................................	469	14.95	_____
_____	Victory Beer Recipes	467	11.95	_____
_____	Winners Circle	464	11.95	_____

CLASSIC BEER STYLE SERIES

QTY.	TITLE	STOCK #	PRICE	EXT. PRICE
_____	Pale Ale	401	11.95	_____
_____	Continental Pilsener	402	11.95	_____
_____	Lambic...	403	11.95	_____
_____	Oktoberfest, Vienna, Märzen.........................	404	11.95	_____
_____	Porter	405	11.95	_____
_____	Belgian Ale	406	11.95	_____
_____	German Wheat Beer......................................	407	11.95	_____
_____	Scotch Ale	408	11.95	_____
_____	Bock	409	11.95	_____
_____	Stout	410	11.95	_____

PROFESSIONAL BREWING BOOKS

QTY.	TITLE	STOCK #	PRICE	EXT. PRICE
_____	Brewery Planner	500	80.00	_____
_____	North American Brewers Resource Directory....	506	100.00	_____
_____	Principles of Brewing Science	463	29.95	_____

THE BREWERY OPERATIONS SERIES, Transcripts
From National Micro- and Pubbrewers Conferences

QTY.	TITLE	STOCK #	PRICE	EXT. PRICE
_____	Volume 6, 1989 Conference...........................	536	25.95	_____
_____	Volume 7, 1990 Conference...........................	537	25.95	_____
_____	Volume 8, 1991 Conference, Brewing Under Adversity.................................	538	25.95	_____
_____	Volume 9, 1992 Conference, Quality Brewing — Share the Experience	539	25.95	_____

BEER AND BREWING SERIES, Transcripts
From National Homebrewers Conferences

QTY.	TITLE	STOCK #	PRICE	EXT. PRICE
_____	Volume 8, 1988 Conference...........................	448	21.95	_____
_____	Volume 10, 1990 Conference.........................	450	21.95	_____
_____	Volume 11, 1991 Conference, Brew Free or Die!..........	451	21.95	_____
_____	Volume 12, 1992 Conference, Just Brew It!	452	21.95	_____

SUBTOTAL _____

Call or write for a free Beer Enthusiast catalog today.
• U.S. funds only.
• All Brewers Publications books come with a money-back guarantee.
*Postage & Handling: $4 for the first book ordered, plus $1 for each book thereafter. Canadian and international orders please add $5 for the first book and $2 for each book thereafter. Orders cannot be shipped without appropriate P&H.

Colo. Residents Add 3% Sales Tax _____

P&H * _____

TOTAL _____

Brewers Publications, PO Box 1510, Boulder, CO 80306-1510, U.S.A.; (303) 546-6514; FAX (303) 447-2825

We're here for your beer!

No, we don't want to take your homebrew away from you (although we'd be glad to sample a few bottles). We at the American Homebrewers Association® want to help you brew the best beer in the world — your own. For more than 18 years we've helped homebrewers of every level brew fantastic beer at home. Whether you're a beginner or an advanced fermentologist, we'll be there for you. (If that means drinking some of your homebrew, all the better.)

MEMBERSHIP BENEFITS INCLUDE:

Five big issues of Zymurgy® magazine

Discounts on entries at the annual AHA National Homebrewers Conference

Discounts at the annual AHA National Homebrew Competition

Discounts on select books from Brewers Publications

The Homebrew Club Network

The Members-Only Tasting at the Great American Beer Festival®

Free information for better homebrew

Discounts to AHA Sanctioned Competitions

Members Information Service

Your membership also supports the AHA's educational programs, the new Beer Evaluation Program and the state-by-state AHA Homebrew Legalization Campaign.

The American Homebrewers Association is your partner in better homebrewing.

"I read it in *The New Brewer.*"

**Jerry Bailey, President,
Old Dominion Brewing Co.,
Ashburn, Va.**

I ndustry leaders like Jerry Bailey know that only *The New Brewer* provides the inside information craft brewers from coast to coast depend on. Each issue is packed with vital statistics for business planning, the latest in brewing techniques, alternative technologies, beer recipes, legislative alerts, marketing and distribution ideas — everything you need to succeed in today's competitive market.

Whether you're an established brewery or just in the planning stages, our in-depth coverage will give you information you can put to work immediately. After all, your business is our business.

See for yourself. Subscribe to *The New Brewer* today!

The **New Brewer** · YOUR INSIDER'S VIEW TO THE CRAFT-BREWING INDUSTRY